WHAT THE EARLY WORM GETS

WHAT THE EARLY WORM GETS

Scott Stevens

Library of Congress Control Number:		2010912953
ISBN:	Hardcover	978-1-4535-6978-8
	Softcover	978-1-4535-6939-9
	Ebook	978-1-4535-6979-5

Follow WHAT THE EARLY WORM GETS at AlcoholAuthor on Twitter.
whattheearlywormgets@gmail.com.

This book was printed in the United States of America.

To order additional copies of this book, contact:
Xlibris Corporation
1-888-795-4274
www.Xlibris.com
Orders@Xlibris.com
86169

ACKNOWLEDGEMENTS

To the Wisconsin Department of Corrections, Massachusetts Department of Correction, Texas Department of Criminal Justice, Florida Department of Corrections, all the researchers and authors, biological anthropologists, alcohologists and geneticists mentioned in this book, and the dedicated Alcoholism professionals of the organizations accredited by the Joint Commission on Accreditation of Healthcare Organizations. Thank you for providing the facts upon which this book is founded.

LML. LKS. Kyle. Amy Jo. Sue. Trish. Hawk. Julani. Leonard. Alcoholics Anonymous. The Law Offices of Andrew Mishlove. Dr. Linda Williams. Valley Hope Chandler and Tempe . . . thanks more than you can ever imagine. Gemma and the people at Xlibris. Mom. Sister. Uncle Mark. Aunt Jill and Uncle Bob. Aunt Irene and Uncle Jim. The mother of my children. The kids the kids the kids. Without you, love would be loveless, meaning would be meaningless, dreams would be pointless and hope—no kidding—would have been hopeless.

FOREWORD

"The 'Good Creature of God,' it is given to children for many ills of childhood.

"Its wholesomeness in health only surpassed by its healing properties in case of disease. No other element is capable of satisfying so many human needs.

"It contributes to the success of any festive occasion and it spirits those in sorrow, gives courage to the soldier, blesses the traveler with endurance, grants foresight to the statesman and inspiration to the preacher. It sustained plowman, trader, trapper and sailor."

—*J. Krout, "The Origins of Prohibition" 1925, Knopf, NYC*

And it kicked my butt.

It drives our healthcare system to near collapse.

It racks up $220 billion a year in social and health costs. That's more than obesity or cancer, according to the National Center on Addiction and Substance Abuse's 2005 data.

There is a basic disconnect that rules where we are today in terms of the legal treatment of alcohol-related crimes. Our system was founded on Malum in Se (crimes that are wrong in and of themselves, like theft and murder) and Malum Prohibitum (crimes we deem as crimes for public welfare). We're now treating both the same, and treating sick people as criminals.

This isn't an I-came-to-Jesus-so-you-should-too conversion tale. I'm Christian, not that it is your business.

It isn't temperance-oriented drivel advocating a return to Prohibition. The United States has lapsed back into half-heartedly jousting with alcohol-related problems—research, treatment or prevention—gradually back-burnering the issue not long after Lyndon B. Johnson declared it a "national priority" in 1966. No broadly conceived program on prevention or treatment exists today even if we are smarter than we were in '66. Smarter, but not wiser. Tax dollars are being fumbled between criminal justice and healthcare systems.

And even the Treasury, which counts alcohol tax income as the nations third-largest revenue source, struggles with how alcohol taxes rub up against the social cost of drinking.

WHAT THE EARLY WORM GETS isn't a political manifesto. Nor is this a beef about the overburdened Corrections system—although the fact that Corrections needs fixing isn't breaking news. Just remember that exactly half of people trained for ANY job are below average. That's the definition of average after all. Probably one in three administrators could be jettisoned without "endangering the public," but I don't have the will to challenge the Corrections patronage and mechanisms between the covers of this book. After seeing what I've seen in two years' incarceration, we *do* need more guards and better trained ones. Believe it or not, there are some officers who still think Andersonville is a pretty good model for interring felons, but most of them are good, hard workers. I used to think they were all misery pimps, but began to accept that statement about "average" was really truth and—besides—a goodly percentage of the felons bring the ignorance and heavy handedness on themselves. That doesn't grant officers permission to some of the strange ideas of self importance they'll take out on inmates. (Or were some of us actually "patients?") And it certainly doesn't grant a right to Corrections officials to determine who needs "help" when they don't know themselves.

Access to real treatment from general hospitals and treatment centers needs to improve because the humane and effective help is out of reach for most people. Until we begin holding a telethon for Smirnoff's Kids as we do for Jerry's Kids, a better allocation of existing treatment dollars has to be a desirable and reachable goal.

I'm your neighbor. That's what compelled me to essay. I'm not the outdated stereotype Americans pin to Alcoholics. I'm the quiet neighbor with the polite kids . . . the neighbor who keeps his lawn mowed and his home kept up. I'm a man of many desks in a long and successful career. Not blue collar, but not blueblood either. I have two degrees. I had one wife for most of my adult life. I'm the respected community leader, even if I don't always lead the opinions in my own house. I'm behind you in church on Sunday morning and in the foursome in front of you at the course Sunday afternoon.

Alcohol and the trouble I landed in were not in my plans. Nor is jail a right of passage for my family or my neighborhood. So perhaps my story and my perspective on the difference between Alcohol Abuse and Alcoholism have an angle you can use. I learned a surprising amount about that difference in treatment, and among the antisocials with whom I had to live, because I drank and drove.

My life accomplishments have been pretty normal peppered with outstanding experiences like meeting seven Presidents of the United States, flying with the Navy's Blue Angels, piloting a Los Angeles Class nuclear sub and driving a NASCAR over 140 mph. Most importantly, my children respect me and like me as well as love me. Not any of the experiences I had before or the things I accomplished in the lifetime before six disastrous weeks prepared me for the last few years. The experience I came through might surprise you to find out that the kind of coercion that might be common in China goes on every day in 21st century America.

I do want to make it abundantly clear that in no way am I NOT guilty of drinking and driving. That doesn't make me anymore of a sociopath than a U.S. President who lied about smoking pot. In fact, last I checked that is illegal, too.

Your tax dollar is being squandered on ineffective so-called treatment programs as a result. In this day of governmentalized health care, you're also now in an insurance pool with more Alcohol Abusers than ever before and they account for the single highest proportion of health care costs because of the havoc alcohol creates in an otherwise physically healthy human specimen. You will be fortunate to not get caught in the Corrections vortex. You *are* caught up, though, in the failures of the treatment system that very often gets colored through the lenses of our individual beliefs about Alcohol Abuse and Alcoholism.

For example, sometimes the opinion we have of the alcoholic gets mated up with a hard-partying-frat-boy-who-won't-grow-up mentality. Or brown-bag wino Skid Road types. I was neither of those. Instead I was a driven executive who secretly devoured two liters of booze a day and got four drinking and driving arrests in six weeks. (It *is* road, not row, by the way. Skid Road, a track down which logs were skidded to a lumber mill in Seattle where the lumberjacks usually passed out on Fridays, not Skid Row, another nickname for Cannery Row. It took me five digits worth of private rehab to learn that tid-bit.)

Here I'm giving the facts as they relate to science and as they relate to experience. Those who have been "inside" will say I am being too light-handed. Those who have never been inside the hell of Alcoholism or the bricks and mortar of another hell, prison, be glad. I hope you get it.

There have been plenty of factual books written about Alcoholism, Alcohol Abuse and incarceration. I'm adding to the body of work, not seeking to replace any of it. I attempt to be as objective of a reporter as I can be, however, I am not detached. I lived it. I cannot be totally removed and make no apology for it. I was the Early Bird who Got the Worm. I was up before every sunrise, day in and day out without fail. And now I know WHAT THE EARLY WORM GETS.

CHAPTER ONE

DECEMBER 15, 2006

Shortly after 4 a.m.

I am up. Never confuse waking up with coming to. I came to a bit earlier than usual. I'm almost always up by 5 a.m. The early bird gets the worm and all, so I'm not unused to seeing this side of the sunrise.

Today's different. I didn't sleep well because the small circular fan my wife of seven months uses as white noise wasn't running. I'd become accustomed to the white noise so I missed it. It wasn't there because she wasn't there. She was at her boyfriend's and didn't come home. She's pissed. And cheating. Bad combo. It's easy to see why with all the drinking I was doing. Accepting that doesn't make it hurt me any less. There would be no wake-up sex in this house today. No make-up sex either. Not this time.

The drinking and driving arrest I got two afternoons ago no doubt was her last straw. But the cheating thing didn't come from that arrest. The cheating was going on for awhile. Since before our wedding (the second for each of us). I don't think I would have ignored it if I wasn't swimming in Jack Daniels every day.

She's not here. I'm still drunk. Neither thing was going to change today.

Our newly remodeled bedroom suite from our beautiful home addition this year was empty except for me and a pint of Jack. I know I crashed at my desk last night, and couldn't tell you how I made it into bed or how I

---

had the smarts to bring the bottle in with me for the eyeopener I have every morning. There were signs of life at the neighbors as bedroom and kitchen lights clicked on throughout our Republican, white-collar neighborhood on Milwaukee's North Shore, just blocks from Lake Michigan. The neighbors would be leaving for work soon this Friday morning. I wasn't.

I took the pint and made my way to the home office down the hall. That's where I kept my laptop, naturally, but also another valuable piece of equipment: A breath-alcohol meter. I booted up the laptop and remember the reading I got while waiting for my Gateway. The reading was .151 I recall because the date was also the 15th and I thought that ironic. I took a huge slug of the whiskey to stave off the horrific shakes I get around .10, which was the reason I bought the meter, to stay ahead of withdrawal.

I knew I had to slam a little more to keep from shaking to pieces as I tried to type in my password and I was sobering. It was like typing wearing a catcher's mitt. I could feel it. And I had a conference call with an East Coast fund manager this morning, so I had to ramp up the Blood Alcohol Concentration to avoid being distracted during the call.

In my calendar I see that I have an open ticket on Midwest Airlines. A headful of whiskey before 5 a.m. told me it would be a good idea to use the ticket. Today. My keys were gone. Same place as my wife. My wallet, too. But I had the open ticket and a limo service that would drop me off at the airport as I've done dozens of times for work.

My closest friend in Phoenix told me to come down when she found out about the arrest Wednesday. I needed to get out of here and wanted so badly to get help. At least I was straight with myself about that. I just wanted to be in treatment there. Two liters of booze day in and day out had me beaten up pretty well.

The flight was at noon. The car would pick me up at 10ish which was perfect because I knew it would be a car with a full bar and by 10 I'd be out of my stashed liquor and panicky. Perfect. No need to sober up at 30,000 feet.

I rocked the conference call which was, more or less, an audition for some speaking engagements I needed so desperately. I haven't worked in awhile. I had a belly full of confidence after that call, plus I was pleased to be leaving Wisconsin December for Phoenix sunshine. That made pumping out a few extra emails really easy. More work related emails, since the fund industry was starting to show the strain that would lead up to the crisis of 2007-2008.

It was a sign, one that I was good at minimizing, that the alcohol was beating me because I was just buzzing when I was typing out such important emails. Just like every day though I *had to* drink. It should also have been a sign two days ago that my BAC was a .312 and I didn't even feel buzzed when the police pulled me over. I even passed two of the roadside sobriety tests at that level. I failed the nystagmus gaze test, which you won't pass intoxicated no matter how high your tolerance is. It should have been a sign that I drank the limo's whole pint of whiskey in the 30 minute drive to the airport. On top of that, I found a hidden liter in a long-forgotten hiding spot and put that in my briefcase and ramped up my Blood Alcohol Concentration to .612. That IS point-six-one-two. It should have been a sign that I came to in a local hospital a couple hours later after airport security couldn't rouse me for final boarding. Should have been a sign, but I was so angry about missing my flight, that I stood up, checked out against medical advice and tried to get the next flight. My BAC was barely under .50 when I came to in that emergency room. I walked out under my own power.

My wife was not running to get me after this caper either. I never made the flight. If I just would have made it to Arizona and rehab that day.

If I just would have made that flight.

Nietzche said, "When you look into the abyss, the abyss looks into you." Well, I peeked into the abyss that day and stared back defiantly. Dumbass. I wasn't at my bottom yet: Worse was still ahead in the next couple weeks.

CHAPTER TWO

"Why am I here, I am not crazy?"
The hatter told Alice, "If you are here, you are crazy. You wouldn't
be here if you weren't."

—*Lewis Carroll, Adventures in Wonderland*

I don't see the humor in calling this a growth experience. But there is something hilarious in what happened when I was arrested for drinking and driving. I was to be punished for the crime, not just for being an inmate, and to "learn my lesson" or probably learn how not to mix alcohol and gasoline. Instead, here are the lessons I learned:

1) Street slang and African American Vernacular English. In a world of malapropisms, missing consonants, poorly conjugated verbs and misused pronouns there is actually a language in it. A Fo-Fo is a .44 magnum . . . deuces are the 22 inch $1,300 rims you have on your $600 car . . . stacks are $1,000 bands of twenty dollar bills . . . and you can have a bitch and a ho and a baby momma and an O.G. (or Ol Gal) and a dime (for a "10" on a scale from one to ten) and they can all be the same female. Don't ax questions. The U. S. Drug Enforcement Agency in August 2010 actually employed nine AAVE

translators if you think I am exaggerating how much the English language is butchered or ignored or both.

2) When your braided hair itches—which is common when you don't wash your hair for six to eight weeks even when you sweat up that nappy mess in the rec yard—you apparently slap yourself repeatedly upside the head because if you scratched it, you'd undo your knots.

3) Light poles are recyclable aluminum and you can get them into a scrap dealer if you cut them up first.

4) There are no garages in the "hood." They were torched a generation earlier for easy insurance money.

5) You can rock up cocaine in ammonia so you don't need heat or flame.

6) You can cheat a urine test with a $250 "whiz-a-nator."

7) When you lift an ATM card or steal it from an unattended mailbox, you go online or to the post office to get the change of address for the statement. When you get the statement, you call and change the PIN. It's like printing your own money.

8) "Golden Roses" gimmicks you get at convenience store checkouts are used as crack vials.

9) You can silently break into a car using a blood pressure cuff to pry open the window, then sliding a stick in to pop the lock.

10) You light a cigarette or a blunt (a hollowed out cigarillo filled with pot) and smoke banana peels in jail by shoving a paperclip in the tip of your electric razor cord, by putting toilet paper in the microwave, or by using your gratis reading glasses as a magnifying glass in the sun. (Did you really think there were that many people reading in jail with that literacy rate?)

11) You can easily use "mother fucker" as any part of speech. It isn't just a noun anymore.

12) A piece of newspaper folded eight times is strong enough to hold back one ton of steel door latch pressure.

13) And never ever burglarize on a Sunday. It's hard to steal the big screen TV when someone is watching it.

Some of this stuff is wildly inventive . . . too bad the brains connected to such cleverness are completely unyoked from any moral compass. My whole life I never met a person with any of this wisdom. Now I am on some kind of campus of crazies where these were the prerequisite courses. Not a bad education for a white collar executive. Micromanagers were the biggest worry of my career and my life, not who was snitching and who was selling in my hood. Culture shock? You bet. I had no expectation of exchanging values, character and intellect. Where was the lesson in sobriety though?

Sensory deprivation is the ONLY way for an educated person to avoid the rampant *anti*-sobriety messages in jail. Not even when I was housed in a minimum-security "treatment" facility. First, the anti-sobriety messaging before I get into the semantics of calling a lock-up a treatment facility. Forty to fifty percent of the time in jail is spent scheming to get drugs or alcohol into jail, planning to deal or drink or get high on the outside on release day, or glorifying how they used drugs and alcohol (and people). This lively chit chat takes place between sleeping and watching cartoons or gambling. The library was a refuge of sorts. The library did have several good books on sobriety and Alcoholism and recovery. The books were not as popular as the Urban fiction or the hip-hop magazines. For example, "Dr. Bob and the Good Oldtimers" is a classic Alcoholics Anonymous book. It was checked out only eight times between 1995 and October 2009 and only once from April 2005 to October 2009.

Sadly, the anti-sobriety messages also were distributed by the program staff at the jail. They permit offenders who had their probation revoked priority access to the taxpayer-funded alcohol programs. These are the same people who failed drug and alcohol tests after already having been released early once! These violators get into programs before a person who is serving his initial incarceration before release. What's more, no priority is given to first-time offenders so a person on his third or fourth or tenth conviction can get into a program. Not once is any priority given to people who actually want to take the publicly funded programs.

Maybe it's just my mainstream, Main Street conservative thinking, but bizarre priority setting such as this with taxpayer dollars seems to be fraught with waste. They will always have the required headcount in those programs. Sometimes inmates cannot even get past the waiting list. Are we fixing the right people?

I struggle with this flawed system because we're told to be sober by people who have no clue what it is like to be Alcoholic, and we're told to succeed in sobriety among people who have no intention of embracing it. We succeed in real recovery when we find a reason—a meaning—in sobriety. In State-run programs you're instructed to be happy when what we really need is a reason to be happy. It's like having your picture taken. You can be told to say, "Cheese." But the great pictures are when the smile is one you had reason to wear.

Corrections is in the role of warehousing humans with varying levels of Antisocial Behavior Disorders. Antisocial is used throughout this essay in its clinical definition which is not a shy or reclusive person but one who has a behavioral disorder leading to repeated offensive and/or illegal activity (and antisocials are anything but shy and reclusive). Sociopaths. Personality disorders. Corrections is in that business. Not in the "treatment" business for a complex medical and biochemical disease like Alcoholism. The judiciary doles out the punishment. The jail's role isn't punishment, it is housing those who are being punished. There is a saying: "You don't go there for punishment, you go there as punishment." Corrections is no more equipped to handle real treatment than an auto mechanic is trained as a French pastry chef. They are two different disciplines. And you wouldn't pay Mr. Mechanic for his cooking. But you are paying billions for ineffective programs run by Corrections with your tax dollars with sometimes toxic results.

Perhaps a better result would come from the officials to subcontract out to health and social services professionals to handle programs and treatment since they are responsibilities well beyond the scope of warehousing felons. The armed services subcontracts to Halliburton to run kitchens and bathrooms and generators and copy machines so forward troops don't have to do these things and focus on their primary responsibility of fighting.

The bottom line is that violent and career criminals need to be locked up, and for a long time. But Pew research shows that prisons are housing too many people who can be managed safely and held accountable in the community at far lower cost under house arrest, and without costly programming the Corrections machine is not qualified to present. Other miscreants of similar demeanor, such as tax or securities cheats, often do get house arrest with a couch and a sofa . . . and internet connectivity from which they could conceivably reoffend . . . while a person with an illness recognized by the AMA gets hard time for a criminal traffic offense and no other assaultive convictions.

In an exit interview the program director for the Corrections alcohol program I was in admitted two things. She said, "This is the only exposure most inmates get for alcohol problems," and in practically the next sentence added, "On average a person has 13 programs before sobriety." Not recovery, but sobriety. I don't think these two facts are unrelated. If they go through 13 programs, you pay 13 times, and we may be paying the wrong facilitators.

Here's another saying: "The jail's job is to make sure you don't come out the other end more pissed off than when you went in." Jails do call the programs voluntary: You volunteer to take the program or you volunteer for Segregation Status (locked in a single cell 23 hours per day with no TV or radio). That's coercion. Institutionalized bullying. It didn't work in WWII when a "work or fight" bill would've forced absentees who didn't want to fight in Europe or the Pacific to work for Navy contractors. That would have bought a Navy full of bitter and unmotivated recruits, not the patriotic veterans we have.

Coercion ignores centuries of experience with career criminals. Corrections should know more than any other profession about the Semantic Aphasia most felons master: They will tell you what you want to hear—that they want the program—when they have no desire to be in the program because doing the program means not going to Segregation and/or maybe getting out earlier. That generates the hostility and ratchets up the pissed off factor.

CHAPTER THREE

"Once you are a pickle, you cannot go back to being a cucumber."

—AA saying

A Correctional Treatment Facility is 100 percent correctional. No treatment takes place here. With the odd priorities mentioned previously, you could make the argument that this is *mistreatment* not treatment. And just how many treatment centers have guards and razorwire. YOU feel better thinking the billions you spend on these campuses are hard at work though, but the accountability and results just do not support that good feeling. And there is another reason for the name on the razorwire fence.

Corrections is business. As a privatized industry it is wildly profitable. As a governmental unit, the Corrections Department is fighting for more dollars. By putting "Treatment" in the name on the gate, and running the programs, the Department gets Federal grants. These are used to offset the per head cost of incarceration. The programs are not monitored for effectiveness or results because they don't have to be. The inmates in the programs are coerced into them and the state is repaid by Washington, DC for each person attending, not for each one who stays out of jail. In Wisconsin, in 2009, the per head cost is $79.45 per inmate per day. ($52 per day in Florida, $21.28 per day in Alabama, $123.28 per day in Rhode Island . . . the national average is $65.41 per day . . . probation/parole or community supervision costs $5 to $25 per day depending upon GPS and or SCRAM use) Without the program reimbursement from the government, which mainly comes from the U.S. Department of Health and Human Services, the cost balloons. That's the cost for all inmates even though not all inmates will have a slot in the program.

These are programs . . . behavioral programs . . . not medical treatment. Treatment—*only appropriate treatment appropriately administered*—is going to achieve the goal of getting an Alcoholic better. The Alcohol Abuser might benefit from the programming since Alcohol Abuse is a behavior problem, not the disease. However, in neither case is forcing a person into treatment any more ethical than denying a person treatment.

If prison treatment facilities are indeed medical, there would be some element of informed consent. And there cannot be a penalty like going to Segregation or losing early release eligibility for withdrawing consent for the procedure.

Reality has very little to do with jail behavioral programs and they bear very minimal resemblance to similar behavior modification programs in the community. Politicians create programs. Not doctors. Because the programs are not for the inmate. The programs are for the public and the politicians who think the inmate will be less of a threat to the public if forced to take the program. The program is for the voter, not the inmate, to neutralize how dysfunctional you think the sociopaths are going to be upon getting out. Because we're tough on crime.

The state purchases the program. They are not developed in house. The doctors and social workers and counselors on state payroll are generally competent, but recovery experts they're not. The states purchase packages from AR Phoenix Resources and Hazelden and a handful of other vendors to make up for the expertise gap. The square peg doesn't fit the corrections hole though, because the materials assume 1) a *clinical* setting as well as 2) a thorough and accurate assessment of 3) a consenting patient. Then and only then can these programs have maximum effectiveness.

Coerced programming is notoriously flawed from the standpoint that few if any antisocial personality types want to change. Corrections officials acknowledge that, calling it a "challenge." This is a tragedy and a billion dollar waste, not a challenge. Several months of mandatory lectures are not going to change basic temperament. But, boy it does make it look as though we're tough on crime.

Alcoholism is not a crime, by the way, anymore than diabetes or cancer or other illnesses are crimes. Dr. Drew Pinsky, noted alcohologist and addiction doctor in his 2003 HarperCollins book "Cracked," has perhaps the most concise definition I've read: "Alcoholism is a biological disease with a genetic basis plus progressive use in the face of adverse consequences." It's a disease not a crime, which will be further differentiated in another chapter at length. We've somehow criminalized the Alcoholic drinking driver as much as the Alcohol Abuser drunk driver and made them both criminals.

No public official is ever going to run on a soft-on-crime platform. The shell game is that the Federal government is paying the reimbursement for the programs, so the state pols can say they *are* tough and that it doesn't increase, but lowers, the per inmate cost. These funds still come out of your pocket, just a different one. The maximum payback, by the way, from HHS is $800 per week per program enrollee. Compare to the $79.45 per day per inmate incarceration cost. To put it another way, the reimbursement for a six month program is $20,800. The inmate would otherwise cost the state taxpayers $14,421 for six months based on the $79.45 per day. And $22.95 per day if the non-violent offender was on house arrest under his own roof eating his own food, paying his own power bill and seeing a doctor on his own dime.

By the way, those reimbursements are collected by the state before an offender completes the program. Jails don't wait to see if the person returns to jail, they don't even wait to see if they finish the program! And you pay for empty chairs because a slot is not filled with the next inmate on the list.

If it was about treatment and concern, Corrections Treatment Facilities would not have a policy of not shaking hands with inmates. You want me to put my brain and recovery in your hands and you won't even shake mine?

It's about reimbursements. Not rehabilitation. "The Treatment Show" has as much choreography as a Broadway hit, but better financing. Yours.

CHAPTER FOUR

"You can't jump down to the bottom of the stairs in one leap, no matter how much you wish to."

—*Elizabeth Aston, The Exploits & Adventures of*
Miss Alethea Darcy, 2005

C_3H_2OH.

Ethanol.

It works. That's why we use it.

It's that simple and that dangerous.

Alcohol is cheap, legal, accessible and plentiful. Bad day? Have a beer. Good day? Have a beer. Celebrate. Headache. Heartache. Beer. Beer. Beer. Alcohol works. Find one doctor, psychologist, psychiatrist who disagrees. It's extremely important to point out though that there is no such thing as "normal" consumption. We were not built to put this stuff in our systems. Alcohol is toxic. Thus the word in*toxic*ation. Get a drop in your eye once and you'll quickly discover just how irritating it is to the human body. As our body breaks it down, one of the byproducts acetaldehyde is even 30 times more toxic than the alcohol itself. If our livers had nerve endings none of us would ever have a second drink.

I became Alcoholic when I was 38 although the genetic foundation was laid in the womb. I could always hold a beer, but wasn't a partier. (Maybe a little in college.) I had long periods of abstinence and more than a few periods of being overserved. Normal consumption by society's standards anyway. Partying and bingeing just was not congruent with parenthood or the corner office.

Then in 2005 my consumption changed and my body took over. I switched to whiskey one day with no reason other than it worked and it made me urinate less than beer. When my tissues and biochemistry changed with the alcohol, I got terrified. Terrified of withdrawal. I found the bottom very quickly after that compared to some Alcoholics who have two decades of drinking experience before the body imbalance takes charge. For as knowledgeable as I am, I sure was stupid for not seeing that once I got tolerance that should have been the first and final warning to knock it off. I instead found warning sign after warning sign and bottom after bottom. You see, I was still the Early Bird Getting The Worm, despite the constant daily drinking, so everything had to be okay.

I divorced my first wife, engaged my second wife and started a new business venture all in that year. Life had a lot of moving parts but in retrospect many of those moving parts were well lubed with whiskey because I was drinking daily. I was just so terrified of feeling lousy with the shakes I couldn't not drink. My tolerance shot so high so quickly that I literally could not stand up or walk once I *started* to sober up.

Being well thought of in my field, I always took on projects that usually fell to more experienced professionals. I handled so many things so well—on my own—that it was easier to work things out rather than delegate. That was my professional attitude, my outlook toward my hobbies and it was now true for my raging Alcoholism. "I can fix this, too." Another missed warning sign. Instead, my solution was to buy a portable breath tester like the police use so I could keep my BAC over .10 which was the point below which I would start shaking to pieces. I took on that Alcoholism and fixed it alright.

What got me so scared was reading that alcohol is the only chemical withdrawal that can be fatal. Ironically, the thought of death while withdrawing was more terrible to me than drinking myself into a coma or death. Think about it: Alcohol is the ONLY chemical that will disrupt your tissues so much that taking it away from your tissues will kill you. Heroin and other chemicals are highly addictive, frequently cause overdose and make you wish you were dead while detoxing. But the withdrawal itself wouldn't kill you. But alcohol can give you seizure, stroke or heart attack while you put it in your body and when you take it away from a dependent body.

Pain and shakes disrupted my thinking when I didn't have alcohol so I couldn't go there. I had to keep it above .10. The nausea disrupted my thinking more so. Each time I dried out a little I was overcome with waves of the dry heaves. I knew my esophagus was weakened by pouring the booze down straight. All I could picture while I was heaving was bleeding to death from the weak throat's veins rupturing in esophageal vericies, another fatal phenomena suffered in Alcoholics. Death from that is more common than death from cirrhosis for the Alcoholic. Somehow my friend and trusted Counselor Leonard lived through the varicies not once but twice. One of the most beautiful and talented women ever on the LPGA tour almost died of "bleeding out," too. I had no reason to think it was inevitable for me, but I knew it was possible and puking up a continuous blood flow until I bled out was more horrifying than even burning to death.

Not horrifying enough to make me stop, just horrifying enough to make sure I kept drinking to avoid the nausea.

Nobody likes to feel inferior. That kept me miles from getting help until that time I tried to fly to Phoenix. Society equates Alcoholism with failure and weakness, which wasn't consistent with success I was having elsewhere in my life. I didn't even want the humiliation of detoxing safely under medical supervision even though I desperately needed it. From June 28, 2005 on I drank constantly, maintaining .10, hitting bottom after bottom and warning after warning for the next 18 months.

I was doing pretty well, building up my conference speaking calendar. I had a reputation as an expert in retirement planning and I was doing a pretty good job hiding my trouble from others, too. You can hide from others, you cannot hide from yourself. Fact is, I was running around state-to-state. That's escapism. Regular travel is a good escape because you're not seeing the same people daily. If your eyes are a little glassy, well you could just have had a rough flight or a rough night, not Alcoholism. Airplanes, most of them, were a place to drink up. And what do airports have? Bars. And limos? Bars. And hotels? Bars. Even in the room. And if you stop eating, you can bury a lot of liquor in an expense report. It was like being a rock star I guess, and at that point before the recession a lot of people in financial services really believed they *were* rock stars.

I got to a point where I thought I had to stop. But how? I was busy. I was building my own business and my own brand and you just don't take a break from that for rehab. (Unless you are a rock star.) Accomplishment made me more than a little bullheaded, so I continued to pretend like I was Teflon and that as long as I kept up the BAC, all the aches and pains would take care of themselves. I just didn't see hitting a wall. The noise of living large (in my own mind if not in reality) was louder than the noise of dying, which I was.

I had bruises all the time. Big, purple/green/red/black ones. A warning sign that something wasn't right. My liver was working overtime and swollen. I had tingles and radiating paid in my left arm. My heart was not handling the toxin as well. And I was tired, flat out exhausted, all the time. Extensive travel is brutal on a sober body, and downright punishing if you're constantly drinking alcohol. Your body isn't sleeping in Rapid Eye Movement (REM) sleep to rejuvenate and repower yourself because your body's defense systems are in overdrive trying to get rid of poison. The cumulative effect of that sleep deprivation was exhaustion.

But I was never hungover. In fact, I didn't feel drunk. That's why many treatment experts call it drinking and driving rather than drunk driving, because you just don't get a euphoric sensation of feeling drunk when you are that dependent on alcohol. I felt "normal." I was rarely driving so I didn't notice my own impairment. Even when you don't feel it, you *are* impaired, I just wasn't using fine motor skills so I seldom noticed how bad they had to be at that level of consumption. I was clear, not buzzed, and undoubtedly toxic.

By a year later, May 2006, I was having a shot or two just to get downstairs in the morning. My second wife and I married in Mexico for Cinco de

Mayo and I wasn't sober for that day either. I wanted to be so badly, but I was shaking and sweating the whole flight down, that I abandoned any thought of sobering up for the ceremony. Patti knew what was up, too. I wasn't fooling her.

She demanded I stop drinking and threatened separation a couple months later. A few times actually. If I could have, I would have for that woman. Even if she thought her shit was perfume . . . even if the signature of our marriage was how short it lasted. And I would have if I could have for the two amazing kids from my first marriage. My solution instead was to be more secretive about my drinking. Since I was up in the morning before my Mrs., I'd gulp down a couple of drinks before she awoke. I worked from home when I wasn't on the road so all I had to do was white knuckle it until she left for work. Then I'd drink all day until she got home, stashing my empty bottles and the full ones. I'd lost quite a few of them in that process. I'd have a few cocktails with her once she was ready for one after dinner.

Thanksgiving 2006, she was sleeping around though and so I didn't care about how careless I was about exposing my secret drinking. That pissed her off but I wasn't getting behind the wheel so, with no worry of me driving, she only took my cash and credit cards to keep me from drinking. Big mistake.

CHAPTER FIVE

DECEMBER 12, 2006

I was living my life in a high speed chase with Alcoholism. It was gonna stop me if I didn't stop it. Something was bound to happen. Two weeks later, I was driving and I got stopped. Well, actually the truck stopped after I rear-ended a car. It was midday. The only collision on my record. My life went from charmed to all of a sudden it is raining whores and I am the one who'd get hit by a queer. And today as a result I stand out like a boil on a supermodel's backside because I have a record.

I was on a new prescription for my growing depression. It is a chicken/egg thing: The booze could have been feeding the depression or the other way around. Since I denied any alcohol use, my doctor wrote the prescription for lorazepam (related to valium), which I just started the day before. I drank a pint of whiskey on top of my prescription, which I now know was a lethal mix. Even more so mixed with gasoline. Lorazepam is a benzodiazepine which multiplies the effects of alcohol. One benzo + One pint does not equal two, it equals about five times the amount of either substance on its own.

I rear-ended a Jetta hard enough to fire the airbags in my vehicle, which in turn made me swallow a gob of chewing tobacco and retch booze all over the inside of the truck. That was more than enough stench for probable cause.

Thank God I didn't hurt any of the Jetta's passengers because I was driving an F-150 full-size pickup. There is no doubt whatsoever I would have been able to stop the truck in time if my reaction time hadn't been compromised. Without alcohol, that accident would not have happened. But I had a .22 BAC—at noon—and was arrested. Booked. And *released* hours later. The initial court appearance didn't fit on the court docket until after three more arrests in the next six weeks.

After being released, I washed down a couple more benzos, which I recovered from the pickup at the autobody shop, with a liter of whiskey. Two days later, I had the episode in Milwaukee's Mitchell International Airport. By that time I was taking 6mg. of lorazepam daily, which is three times my prescribed daily dose.

That got me into the airport incident of Chapter One a couple days later. Patti and I argued when she finally returned home from the boyfriend's three days following the airport incident. That got me divorce papers and a domestic disturbance call. But I still was not at my bottom. Sadly I never gave the woman a chance to help me or help our marriage because the only time to do that is when you're both sober and I never was. Literally, I hadn't been below .10 for almost a year and a half.

Psychology is amazing but has severe limitations. Even the best professional knowledge and research isn't going to tell you an enormous amount about your darkest days and how you managed them. I can't think of a soul who cannot benefit from counseling because your ignorance about yourself is even larger than your personal knowledge of your darkest days. Self-awareness and self-observation are most difficult of all. That's a good reason why we need help, to see these "blind spots" in our darkest performances. We cannot do that alone.

Thing is, I still wasn't at my bottom. Not even close. Darker performances were ahead.

CHAPTER SIX

"In the dark, all cats are grey."

—*Benjamin Franklin*

The problem with collecting data on drinking drivers is that you only have access to the ones who got caught. Not many are honest either. You will not find one person ever who was arrested the only time he or she drove over the legal Blood Alcohol Concentration (BAC) of .08. A problem is present. But what is the problem?

All drinking drivers may be equal. .08 is .08. The state statutes don't say, "except if you have this condition or that." We're all equal, but we're not the same. And the problem may need a program. It may need treatment. It depends on asking the question, "Is he a problem drinker or does he have a drinking problem?" That difference has been acknowledged by the American Medical Society since 1956. It's a clinical difference and a behavioral one, borne out completely in study after study for sixty years.

If you are a problem drinker (Alcohol Abuser) you aren't automatically an Alcoholic. The gap between is detrimental to addressing either. *An Alcoholic cannot consistently choose to drink or not to drink due to physical dependence, tolerance and altered cellular metabolism.* A drinking problem is the loss of the ability to choose, a problem drinker can still choose but decides to drink anyway. Alcohol Abuse may be a prequel to Alcoholism—an Alcoholic in training maybe—but it is not the same as Alcoholism. This was once called the Disease Concept and was introduced by Dr. E.M. Jellinek in 1960 highlighting FIVE types:

Alpha: the earliest stage of the disease, manifesting the purely psychological continual dependence on the effects of alcohol to relieve bodily or emotional pain. This is the "problem drinker", whose drinking creates social and personal problems. These people can stop if they really want to; thus, do not have a "disease".

Beta: cirrhosis from alcohol without physical or psychological dependence. These are the heavy drinkers that drink a lot, almost every day. They do not have physical dependency and do not have a "disease".

Gamma: involving acquired tissue tolerance, physical dependence, and loss of control. This is the AA alcoholic, who is very much out of control, and does, by Jellinek's classification, have a "disease". Gamma Alcoholics can still choose "when to drink" but not "how much."

Delta: same as Gamma, but with inability to abstain. Delta Alcoholics cannot chose the "when" anymore.

Epsilon: the most advanced stage, manifesting as large quantity drinking, solitary alcohol abuse, with loss of all other interests, endless binges.

Gamma, Delta and Epsilon Alcoholism come chock full of shame, remorse, guilt and self-hate ... Alpha and Beta just don't.

This was called the Disease Concept. It's not a concept anymore, though, any more than we have a world-is-flat concept. Dr. Jellinek's work has been accepted for more than four decades. Misinterpreting the disease by applying the disease label to an Alcohol Abuser (Alpha or Beta above) gives that problem drinker an alibi for failing to make the right choice. Conversely, the last three on the list are not social or psychological dependencies. Searching for a reason why these people drink is superfluous. They drink because they have to.

We've come a long way since the disease was identified. Some credit Dr. Benjamin Rush for calling it a disease as early as the 1800s, but Dr. Jellinek is acknowledged as the one to credit for our modern description. In fact, there is some effort to rename Alcoholism Jellinek's disease, much the way other diseases are named (Lou Gehrig's, Hansen's). That could settle any confusion about the behavioral problem versus the medical problem. Extending the term to Alcohol Abusers is like saying a Rottweiler and a water buffalo are the same since they are both mammals or that a rat and an opossum are the same because they both are ugly, eat garbage and scare girls.

In our overly politically correct 21st century society we've become scared to death to call a spade a spade. A problem drinker is not sick. Don't be squeamish. They are immature and self indulgent. JUST ASK ONE. Those *are* objective definitions, not sugar-coated ones, but not moral judgments either, like wicked or shameful.

One of the top researchers, Don Cahalan wrote "Problem Drinkers: A national survey" (Jossey-Bass) in 1970 based on four studies he authored or co-authored in the 1960s. He said, "Comparing estimates of Alcoholics and problem drinkers is a rather futile exercise because the concepts of Alcoholism and problem drinking are not very similar, do not necessarily apply to the same people and have quite different implications for prevention measures and treatment."

If Alcoholism was a behavioral or emotional or psychological or moral or social or spiritual failing, lab rats would not get Alcoholism, the physiological disease. Rats do not even like alcohol to begin with—so they are incapable of Alcohol Abuse—and haven't the capacity of all of those psychological expressions commonly given as causes for Alcoholism. They are chemically different when Alcoholism is present not morally deficient.

Cahalan and others saw the difference between the Alcoholics and Alcohol Abusers in studies of drinking behavior in the armed services. There's a lot of heavy drinking in the military. You'd expect it in a population consisting largely of young males away from their families and in a stressful environment. Many drank so much that they were at a high risk of developing Alcoholism. Most however only had disciplinary problems, not telltale changes in body tissues. The medical risks and physiology of Alcoholism weren't there. That's why nine of ten people leave Alcoholics Anonymous, the mother of all 12-step programs, in their first year. They walk away saying, "That isn't me." They could be right, too. They could be Abusers not Alcoholics. Yet. And some don't have the physiology to ever get there.

AA co-founder William "Bill" Wilson, in "12 Steps and 12 Traditions," (1981, AA World Services, NYC) wrote that some people "still had their health, their families, their jobs, two cars in the garage. They're scarcely more than potential Alcoholics. Sometimes it is necessary to raise the bottom the rest of us had hit to the point where it would hit them. By going back in our drinking histories we could show that years before we realized it we were out of control and that it was indeed the beginning of a fatal progression."

The Cahalan studies seem to point out, by the way, that while many "grow out of" their binge drinking before becoming physically dependent, a fair, proportionally small number of 50- and 60-year-olds still party and binge until they fall over without ever developing any symptoms of the disease. To put it another way, an Alcoholic says, "never again" and they mean it but cannot stick to it and when an Abuser says, "never again" they don't mean it and will stick to never again only as long as they choose. For some at the Correctional Treatment Facility, they stuck to it only until they got to the parking lot and hoisted a ritual bottle on release day for the rest of the inmates to see from the windows overlooking the parking lot.

Abusers actually have three choices. They can choose not to drink. They can choose to drink moderately. They can choose to get bombed. Freedom of choice. Isn't this the person we should scorn but are less likely to? The person judged and loathed harshly in our culture is the Alcoholic who has no freedom to choose whether or not to drink. Long after we recognized the disease as the problem, not the person, the Alcoholic still gets lumped in with the Abuser. Ignorance.

Too bad there isn't one magic bullet for both Abusers and the Alcoholic. For example, controlled drinking may be a treatment goal for an Abuser. A treatment goal for an Alcoholic though is abstinence. Only abstinence.

Success factors in dealing with either are variables like the client's motivation, severity of drinking, socioeconomic stability and coercion. The largest predictor of success though is an appropriate match between problem and solution. Dr. Marc Schuckit, author of *Alcohol & Sociopathy: Diagnostic Confusion,* in the 1973 "Quarterly Journal of Studies on Alcohol," put it this way. "It is necessary to distinguish between the Alcoholic who engages in a limited sphere of antisocial behavior and of the antisocial who abuses alcohol as part of his behavior. The process and prognosis of these different varieties are distinct." (Ironically, the issue of Dr. Schuckit's article I accessed was in the Corrections's own library, stamped, "Bureau of Program Services." Perhaps they hadn't yet gotten around to reading the 1973 article, as they make no effort to make such a distinction.)

Treatment is like fire. You can cook with it or get burned from it. There are practitioners in the criminal justices system spending your money and burning the daylights out of people with that fire because there isn't an assessment. Only your arrest record. No Alcoholic is going to get well if treated for a behavioral problem instead. No Alcohol Abuser is going to bother seeking help if they'll be treated for a chronic disease they don't yet have and might not acquire. Neither will be helped through coerced programs because, mainly, this is not a passive process.

Nor is it a colorblind one. The realities of race, poverty, class, social isolation, past trauma, sex abuse, sex discrimination and other inequalities all impact a person's capacity for effectively dealing with alcohol's outcomes. Ignore these in an assessment and you're as likely to fail as if you put a person in a program when he has no desire to be there.

The "Diagnostic and Statistical Manual of Mental Disorders, Fourth Edition (DSM-IV) is the clinician's blue book for ailment and assessment of conditions, like Alcoholism, where a cell culture or an MRI are of no value.

Alcohol Abuse is assessed with one or more of these four factors:

- Failure to fulfill roles as a result of drinking
- Recurrent drinking in physically dangerous situations (driving)
- Recurrent legal difficulties
- Continued consumption despite recurrent social/personal problems

Alcohol Dependence is assessed as having three or more of these eight factors:

- Increased tolerance/need more to achieve effect/effects diminished with use of the same amount
- Withdrawal or alcohol consumption to avoid withdrawal
- Alcohol use for prolonged periods and/or in larger amounts
- Persistent desire
- Unsuccessful effort to control/reduce/quit
- Considerable time dedicated to obtaining or using
- Avoidance of social/occupational/recreational activities in favor of use
- Alcohol use continues despite physical problems

For a quarter century the treatment profession has relied on this assessment. Out of statistical necessity, since 16-35 percent of the U.S. population falls into the Alcohol Abuse assessment, materials for programs are geared toward these behavioral issues. Materials for alcohol dependency are non-existent in the jail setting. All inmates in program are subjected to a reorientation of their behavior instead.

There are several other tests administrators use to determine the presence of an alcohol problem, though none are particularly effective at diagnosing or differentiating between the disease and it's counterpart, Alcohol Abuse. A disease on a page is different from a disease in a person and not a single verbal or written test is going to give you the differentiation when someone's freedom is on the line. The cheating is easy.

The CAGE test, goes like this.

- 1. Have you ever felt you should *cut* down on your drinking?
  YES or NO

- 2. Have people *annoyed* you by criticizing your drinking?
  YES or NO

- 3. Have you ever felt bad or *guilty* about your drinking?
  YES or NO

- 4. Have you ever had a drink first thing in the morning to steady your nerves or get rid of a hangover (*eye*-opener)?
  YES or NO

If your early release or seeing your kids was on the line, do you think you could bullshit your way through this test? Just answer "yes" to any single question and the assumption is you are an Alcoholic. You get a program. Bingo, that was easy, see you in six months rather than a year, because who is to say I am lying about my answer?

Another test, another opportunity to BS is called the MAST or Michigan Alcoholism Screening Test. See if you can BS this one to get out a year early:

1. Do you feel you are a normal drinker? ("normal"—drink as much or less than most other people)
   YES or NO

2. Have you ever awakened the morning after some drinking the night before and found that you could not remember a part of the evening?
   YES or NO

3. Does any near relative or close friend ever worry or complain about your drinking?
YES or NO

4. Can you stop drinking without difficulty after one or two drinks?
YES or NO

5. Do you ever feel guilty about your drinking?
YES or NO

6. Have you ever attended a meeting of Alcoholics Anonymous (AA)?
YES or NO

7. Have you ever gotten into physical fights when drinking?
YES or NO

8. Has drinking ever created problems between you and a near relative or close friend?
YES or NO

9. Has any family member or close friend gone to anyone for help about your drinking?
YES or NO

10. Have you ever lost friends because of your drinking?
YES or NO

11. Have you ever gotten into trouble at work because of drinking?
YES or NO

12. Have you ever lost a job because of drinking?
YES or NO

13. Have you ever neglected your obligations, your family, or your work for two or more days in a row because you were drinking?
YES or NO

14. Do you drink before noon fairly often?
YES or NO

15. Have you ever been told you have liver trouble such as cirrhosis?
YES or NO

16. After heavy drinking have you ever had delirium tremens (D.T.'s), severe shaking, visual or auditory (hearing) hallucinations?
YES or NO

17. Have you ever gone to anyone for help about your drinking?
YES or NO

18. Have you ever been hospitalized because of drinking?
YES or NO

19. Has your drinking ever resulted in your being hospitalized in a psychiatric ward?
YES or NO

20. Have you ever gone to any doctor, social worker, clergyman or mental health clinic for help with any emotional problem in which drinking was part of the problem?
YES or NO

21. Have you been arrested more than once for driving under the influence of alcohol?
YES or NO

22. Have you ever been arrested, even for a few hours because of other behavior while drinking?
(If Yes, how many times _____)
YES or NO

SCORING

Please score one point if you answered the following:

1. No
2. Yes
3. Yes
4. No
5. Yes
6. Yes
7. through 22: Yes

Add up the scores and compare to the following score card:

0-2 No apparent problem

3-5 Early or middle problem drinker

6   or more Problem drinker (NOTE: NOT a distinction between problem drinker or drinking problem.)

Even the SASSI, Substance Abuse Subtle Screening Inventory will be fooled by the cons using your money to get out of jail quick. The test was designed, by the way, to fool cheaters. When you are a career antisocial, you are not going to be fooled by the test. I cannot reproduce it here because all SASSI materials are copyrighted and licensed only to trained users by the SASSI Direct, LTD. However, even they claim it is only designed to detect alcohol misuse, not Alcohol Abuse or Alcoholism.

"Adult Psychopathology & Diagnosis" is the text for clinicians especially those in the alcohol dependency and recovery field. It identifies three pillars of getting the assessment right:

1) The assessment is critical to the development of meaningful treatment plans.
2) Accurate diagnosis of alcohol and other concurrent disorders is integral to the assessment process.
3) Ultimately assessment should be determined based on clinical judgment and the patient's needs.

If nobody is arguing with the science that says mixing alcohol with gasoline is a bad idea, then we cannot argue with the science that says assessment is the key to effective treatment.

Believe it or not, there are simple, uncheatable physiological tests that can be performed, but are not. Those enzymatic and blood tests are in Chapter Thirteen. Why do we rely on answers from the patient only, and especially when the budgetary consequences and the healthcare consequences are so high is beyond rational. The fact is, even the most noble among us would cheat his butt off on these tests if it meant minimizing the consequence for an illegal action like driving under the influence. You don't want barbed wire, so lie your tail off.

According to "Addiction Treatment—Avoiding Pitfalls, a Case Study Approach," (Group for the Advancement of Psychiatry, Washington, DC, 1998) there are two problems that exist in non-clinical environments. The first is overdiagnosis: Automatically assuming Alcoholism. The second is not screening for Borderline Intelligence. Borderlines are "apt to be impulsive and resume drinking with minimal stresses before adapting to abstinence. If recovery is based on conceptual models—like Cognitive Behavioral Therapy—the presence of Borderline Intelligence undermines even the best effort."

Here's a better test for Alcoholism that may not predict success in treatment but will give a very definitive assessment: Give yourself one beer/wine/cocktail a day. Want more? Tough. Want to put tomorrow's drink in today's bank? Tough. If you can do this for a period of two weeks, you are not an Alcoholic. Period. I am not uniquely positioned to give medical advice, but I know where I have been and if you fail that test, get help before you go where I have been.

Not making the distinction between problem drinkers and drinking problems among teens or co-workers or drivers is a problem because each distinction involves sanctions which may or may not be appropriate for the problem. (NOTE: I am not saying the distinction is a permit for bad decisions like driving intoxicated or showing up for work with ethanol in the system. But the distinction is important to how you correct the behavior and address the disease if present.)

Jails use none of the three pillars above, nor any of the DSM-IV criteria. The duration of the program is determined by judicial order, the facility you're assigned and why you were arrested and convicted. This information is collated by a $14 per hour Classification Specialist II who never even meets you until the program decision already has been made. No interview. No questionnaire. There's hardly even an educational evaluation to determine if offenders can keep up with the reading-intensive behavior modification program. If you can read a list of 10 words, you can read. Although the AR Phoenix Resources website states their materials are prepped for a fourth-grade reading level, that 10-word, one-minute test is all that's required. GED/HSED/Diplomas are not verified until after the program begins. (They twice asked for my GED. I have a Master's.) One of my program groupers asked me to spell the following words as we did our homework in a single two-hour session: Duty, Apply, Early, Steel, Own, Pay, Speak, Guide, Drunk, Caught, Path, Anger, Stole, Effect, Group, Shop, Heard, Friends, Truth . . . and more . . . 43 words in all. Sufficient evidence this inmate was never given the Test of Adult Basic Education (TABE) required of all inmates serving longer than a year . . . and he apparently was not administered the test on any of his other FOUR incarcerations.

You're slotted a bed date, one size fits all. Your conviction is actually the least influential of the factors. Bed space is often the main decision point. One roommate of mine—an armed robber—got into the program, 16 years after his conviction only because he was high at the time of that robbery. A second roommate—this one a deadbeat dad on a two year child support sentence—also was allowed in the program.

A Muslim, he doesn't drink.

CHAPTER SEVEN

"Beware the fury of a patient man."

—*John Dryden*

In the northern hemisphere, we have decades of good science and results in both alcoholism and its treatment. The State has its rules however, and leveraging the best treatment knowledge of a disease that has no rules, has no place in the world of the State's rules.

The oldest written rules, The Code of Hammurabi, date back 3,800 years. Two hundred eighty two rules carved on a seven foot rock. The Ten Commandments are newer by more than five centuries. Humans have always needed rules to prevent disorder. However, in the criminal justice system, some rules are created to preserve disorder.

The term META RULES describes the rules or commands that supersede all other rules you've gotten. In America, the meta rule superseding the Bill of Rights is called In The Interest of National Security. In the Bible, the meta rule over the Ten Commandments is John 13:34, Love One Another. In childhood the meta rule over *anything* is Mom Said So.

Once introduced to coerced alcohol programming, the meta rule superseding any treatment protocol or science developed over the history of the disease of Alcoholism is The State Said So. The Classification Specialist II cannot be wrong. Their data on your arrests is frighteningly frequently paired with the wrong offender, missing or just plain wrong but the program you get as a result of that arrest record is the right program. The State Said So. There is an appeal process. Not surprisingly, it is also in the Classification Unit. No rational person would allow his mother-in-law to be arbiter of a marital dispute.

The state also determines that you volunteer for the program, or volunteer to lose your license permanently. You're not eligible for early release from incarceration or probation if you don't volunteer. And if you're incarcerated, you volunteer to work in Dante Algheri's fourth circle of hell, the jail kitchen, if you do not volunteer for the program. The State Said So.

Never confuse compliance with treatment.

The chart below began in 1967 by the Alcohol Council of Greater Los Angeles and is the most effective, at-a-glance illustration the true treatment industry has to demonstrate the scope of Alcohol Abuse and Alcoholism, dependency and recovery. I've seen a version from Hazelden, the renowned treatment facilities. And the best counselor I ever witnessed, Hawk, also had his own version. The chart I included here has my own embellishments as well.

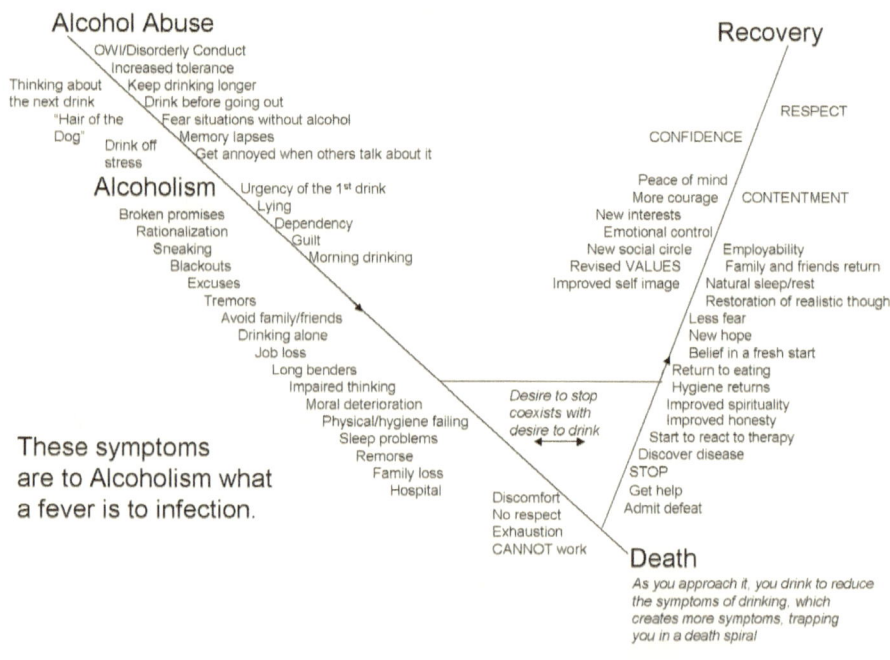

A criminal justice program is an off-the-shelf solution to only one small entry on the upper left of the chart, "OWI/Disorderly Conduct." Compliance with their program allegedly prevents offenders from reoffending, not from sliding down the entire left side of the illustration. The scope of Alcohol Abuse and Alcoholism is much greater than one single entry on the downward progression. An Alcohol Abuser can and often does progress past that phase as discussed last chapter, though not always all the way down the left slope.

It's important to note that not all the symptoms or signs on the left will manifest themselves, just like some of the DSMIV criteria won't apply to every Alcoholic. They might not appear in that order either. You can move down the left swiftly or slowly. However it is a down escalator. Alcoholism follows this as an agenda. It does not comply with a political agenda. You can, however, jump from the left to the right side and jump back to the left again. The alcohol will determine that for you.

You don't have to be at the bottom of the left before beginning recovery. I was though. The intro to the book wasn't my bottom. We'll get to that in later chapters. Forcing compliance with not drinking does NOT constitute recovery or get you to the right side for long. Alcohol doesn't care that the State Said So.

Surrender is what gets a person to the right side of the chart. It's the difference between compliance and recovery. Unfortunately, surrender is not a goal of a coerced program, only compliance. Psychiatrist Harry Tiebout, prominent in the middle of the last century, often wrote of compliance vs. surrender. Surrender is an acceptance, intellectually and emotionally. Only when you surrender to the fact that you cannot control alcohol once you become Alcoholic, says Tiebout, can you move from the left to the right with permanence. Compliance can get you over there, only surrender can keep you there. That's why "Detox" is after surrender on the progression up the right side. Detox can even happen briefly on the left during hospitalization. Three weeks later, often longer, after detox, your body is still fighting off the toxicity though. Without surrender, without real, voluntary treatment, the Alcoholic goes back to alcohol before the cells and tissues have entirely detoxified. Later chapters discuss the biochemistry.

When I decided to surrender and believe my life was unmanageable and dangerous, it was only the start of a really long road that has a speed limit and cannot be shortened. A person enters therapy insisting he wants to change. Nobody wants to change really. What you really want is to remain the same and have therapy make you feel better. Nothing wrong with that. It's a human failing common to all humans, not just the ones who want to accept it. It does connect well with the idea of surrendering and allowing therapy to start working. Whichever therapy you choose. (As long as you have the choice.)

It doesn't matter which one is best or biggest or first. It is surrendering and getting into an appropriate mode of treatment that matters. The problem a lot of Alcoholics face early on is that we're leaves who don't think we're part of a tree. "I'm unique." Surrender acknowledges that we're not so unique and this chart applies to everyone with the disease. To play off the metaphor a little more, the State wants to make you all leaves whether you're an Abuser or Alcoholic. They put all these different leaves on the same tree whether you are an oak or a plastic ficus at Walmart.

Another of my embellishments to the chart is the point at the bottom of the chart where recovery and disease intersect. From either side you can feel the need to quit. You can feel, "If I keep drinking I'll die" simultaneously to feeling, "If I don't have one right now I'll die." It's like the rumble strip on the roadway between the lane and the ditch: You'll hit the rumble strip both on your way to the ditch and on your way back to the road.

You see on the right, guilt and shame are a large part of Alcoholism and successful treatment regimens seek to disarm the guilt/shame an Alcoholic accumulates. That's what the "Death Spiral" is about in part. There is a biological feeding frenzy when you're that close to death, that close to the bottom. The body needs more alcohol, more of the same substance that is killing it. Guilt and shame play a role in feeding that spiral because the more you drink, the more guilt you build and the more shame others heap on you so you drink even more. Since criminal justice programs are designed to increase your shame to get you into compliance, it is no wonder they are ineffective, especially for the late-stage Alcoholic. Corrections deals with guilty people and uses that guilt to shame people, most of whom are incapable of shame. Treatment actually deals with alleviating shame. Corrections and treatment are not congruent.

"Shame, The Power of Caring," by Gershen Kaufman, (Schenkman Publishing, Cambridge, Mass. 1980) describes shame as "the most poignant experience . . . whether felt in humiliation or cowardice or in a sense of failure to cope successfully with a challenge." That's what criminal justice programs are designed to foster: Shame for not coping successfully if you ever drink again.

In successful rehabilitation a lot of time is dedicated to defining guilt—I did bad—and separating it from shame—I am bad—and *eliminating* shame as a tool to keep you in sobriety. Criminal justice seeks to remind you that you are bad for getting on that downward slope to begin with even when you are on the upslope. As you'll see later, an Alcoholic literally has no say in the downward progression once he or she starts drinking. In fact, the middle steps of AA's 12 steps focus on cleaning house and getting rid of guilt and shame, not building it.

Incidentally, battling grief and its five stages is also critical to AA and to moving from the left of the chart and staying on the right. You create a lot of grief in the later stages on the left. The five stages of grief are denial, anger, bargaining, depression and acceptance according to Elisabeth Kubler-Ross in "On Death & Dying" (MacMillan, NYC 1969). They must be dealt with to fight against the disease that caused the grief. Each of the five is a personal process, not a workbook chapter or a video lesson to be covered in a program. The environment of a jail, the inmates and the staff, quite possibly are the worst grief support community I can think of.

My Corrections program group the facilitator actually referred to as a community. Delaware's Key-Crest, Amity in California, Cornerstone in Oregon, New Vision in Texas and Stay-n-Out in New York also start out with the same fundamental mistake. To me, the gangster racists in the group wouldn't call this a community with me in the fold, any more than I consider them part of my community. I personally associate with culturally literate professionals, intellectuals and taxpayers who accomplish and achieve and don't use illegal drugs. I tend to value morals, too. That's who I can grieve and recover among. The other members of my community had none of those qualifications and no interest in healing of any sort, instead preferring to chill with gold-toothed manchildren in the rec yard with their pants hanging down off their butts. The State Said So, so this is my community.

There was no educational assessment to make certain the community progressed at the same pace . . . no socio-economic screen to make our stories more relevant to each other . . . and no measure to even find how motivated the participants were in relation to each other. Offenders aren't even divided up between drug dealers, chemical and Alcohol Abusers, and Alcoholics. Antisocial personalities and Alcoholics were equal *and the same*. Don't cure a personality disorder some offenders don't have. And don't waste money on and threaten to undo the healing which some already began before being incarcerated. (For example, I voluntarily went to private rehab before my sentence, which wasn't rehab considered by the State.)

I paid for treatment. I made the commitment including the financial one, voluntarily, for inpatient rehabilitation in Chandler, Arizona in 2007. Insurance didn't cover it for me because I was uninsured but most insurance does provide coverage for Alcoholism treatment. The insurance company wants to see a DSM-IV diagnosis of Alcoholism. The provider 1,400 miles and two time zones away requires a signed Health Information Privacy (HIPAA) release for the facility to release to the State information pertaining to my completion of treatment. The State however refused to accept the confirmation without the facility signing the *State's* version of the HIPAA release, even though the State was not the one releasing the information. So you paid for my State program even after I had already completed treatment out of my own pocket once.

That mentality can work for punishing an Alcohol Abuser, not for treating an Alcoholic because Alcoholics only get the treatment when the alcohol says so, not when the State Says So. By the way, that's where comparison to the disease of diabetes fails, because a diabetic will follow through with treatment when a doctor recommends it. The public danger of

—

diabetics not following through is no lower than when an Alcoholic doesn't get treatment.

When the State Says So isn't the same as when a clinician says so. The consequence is that people are slotted in an alcohol program ill-suited for their needs. Unwilling people take up space in a program. People are placed in the same program they may have completed on 12 prior incarcerations. Public funds are squandered in this kind of bureaucratic arrogance, this kind of meta rule.

Two other considerations of this meta rule. First, it discriminates against offenders controlling depression and other mental disorders with prescription medication. Second, the State program ignores a simple, free and proven resource for keeping people off alcohol since 1935, Alcoholics Anonymous, in favor of the program the State purchases.

The discrimination against those treating depression will catch up with States first. Presently, offenders are given a mental health score ranging from MH0 to MH3. MH0 means a person has no mental health issues. Offenders can go to any facility, even work release facilities which allow minimum security offenders out into the community for as much as 60 hours per week. MH3 is considered mental retardation. MH1 and MH2 are varying degrees of mental health concerns from depression to bipolar disorders currently being treated with prescription drugs under the care of a physician. When depression or anxiety medications or other psychotropics are dispensed, a MH1 or MH2 can only be given a bed date at a facility with a health services unit, never a work release facility. The trouble is twofold. Inmates deliberately under-report depression or other mental health issues because they want to go to a work release facility. You'll only make pennies per hour working inside a facility, compared to earning at least minimum wage in the community. What's even more frightening is that offenders who are on medication stop taking them to get into a work release site six months later. Who is less danger to the community? A schizophrenic off his meds and counseling so he could get MH0? Or a person with mild depression under a maintenance dosage of anti-depressants?

The other problem is that alcohol programs are fewer, with fewer bed dates, at facilities that accommodate MH1 and MH2 classifications because the classroom space is taken up partially by the health services unit. So offenders are penalized for having depression by having to wait longer for a program which they're told they must have but might not fit their needs. Or you let depression go untreated so you can get a program bed date sooner and possibly go home sooner.

(Here's another little known but related fact, you can get to a work-release facility only if you complete your program first. Doesn't that speak volumes about how sincerely willing people are to discover "recovery" in the program? Many are just there merely to go through the motions in a program so they can get rubber stamped so they can get to a work release and see their babymomma!)

The State ignoring AA is also a financial burden. In the history of programs (AA is not treatment), 12 step programs have saved millions of lives, millions of families and billions of health care and corrections dollars. It works. It is NOT for everyone, but it works. There are other programs, too, however AA is in about every locale in which an offender will be in while incarcerated or when released. Starting an inmate who wants to change with 12 step work while incarcerated, then transitioning to the same 12 step work on the outside seems like a common sense way toward the goal of reducing recidivism. It's ignored or so limited by the State as to be ineffective in jails.

AA has been labeled a spiritual or spirituality based program and that drives the State's lingerie into a tight knot because "spiritual" is close to "religious." AA is spiritual ... if you make it that way. Astoundingly, Robin Casarjian's faith-based (aka spiritual) healing program for prisoners called "Houses of Healing" was produced and written with the Massachusetts Department of Correction and is a primary AODA program read.

In Wisconsin, you do not have AA meetings in prisons, due in part to a lawsuit from an inmate who claimed you cannot coerce me into a program AND have it be religious. So instead of stopping the coercion, the State stopped AA. They do not even have it in the "treatment facilities." They do offer a meeting that uses the famous "Big Book" of Alcoholics Anonymous. If you're in program, you must attend, you sign in and prison staff must be present. Sort of takes the Anonymous part away and it's hardly a supportive support group if attendees are there because they have to be, not because they want to be. Predictably, if you force someone to go, it will be less successful. In one February 2009 class, from which they turned offenders away at the door because it was overcrowded, I ratted out a fool who brought a library book and was reading it IN THE MEETING.

Courts have ruled on the constitutionality of mandatory 12-step programs. Two appeals courts and two state high courts have said it violates the 1st Amendment by requiring attendance. Circuit courts, mind you, still require it in pretrial intervention systems, weaseling around the 1st Amendment argument by saying it is a pretrial option and voluntary. If you don't volunteer, you get a stiffer sentence. The Supreme Court of the United States has never ruled on mandatory 12-step programs, although several such appeals have come to it for review.

Some crafty criminals and attorneys also say it violates the 8th Amendment banning cruel and unusual punishment because they don't want the program. That argument always loses steam based on the simple fact that just because you think it is personally unpleasant does not make it cruel or unusual.

As evidence that an astronomically high percentage of offenders do not really want any kind of help, one facility I visited (not of the treatment variety) housed 1,400 offenders. One non-mandated quasi-AA meeting a week was attended by three offenders, including me. At least they were there for the correct reason: Because they wanted it. They surrendered. They want to stay on the right half of the chart.

The Chaplain must approve your attendance in advance if a 12-step is in place, even though AA is non-denominational. The participants in the meetings-not-to-be-confused-with-AA are asked to leave immediately following the meeting, if they are allowed entry. Offenders in the treatment facility offered meetings are routinely turned away because they only offer a single meeting per week, and if you're required to go, the seating fills quickly.

Turned away from a mandatory AA meeting? AA co-founder Wilson said, "We can always make room for a drunk."

The meetings are chaired by an AA from local chapters. After leaving rehab in 2007 and before starting my sentence in late 2008 I was active with my AA "home group's" Hospitals and Institutions outreach which go into jails and general hospitals to talk about sobriety. We were not informed that those in our meetings had to sign in or that people were required to attend and sometimes turned away. It would not have changed the message we brought, but it would have convinced us to have a second meeting for people who weren't just page turners or pretenders any longer.

Did I mention AA is free? Only the State could have the arrogance to think their expensive program—the one you fund—is better than a free one with a proven success rate, which is the program used in conjunction with 90 percent of the nation's voluntary treatment facilities.

As for the God or god factor, your tax dollar provides for Bible studies, Koran studies, Native American sweat lodge ceremonies, Ramadan meals. A higher power seems evident in each of these, certainly more so than in AA. Terrorist Michael Finton, who in 2009 planned to blow up an Illinois Federal building, first attended a taxpayer funded religious conversion program *while behind bars* to become Muslim and join the jihad. But he would have had a harder time attending AA behind bars.

I'm not a shill of AA. I believe it works for me, have a sponsor, attend meetings. It also has a better reputation and results than the State programs. AA works *despite* religion actually because many more than attend are scared off by misinformation about AA's spiritual roots. There's no worship, only fellowship. It doesn't require you to do anything, only to have a willingness to stop drinking. You can have a God or a god or nothing. AA doesn't fit the meta rule of the State, so you're missing out on the benefit of an effective, time-honored program.

Treatment experts pro-AA and anti-AA agree that step one of the 12 is not spiritual. Step one is "We admitted we were powerless over alcohol and that our lives had become unmanageable." So what would be the harm in letting offenders get to step one and making their own informed decision?

There's a man who wrote his son on and off over a year about two horses he could not tell apart. He cut one's mane. "That worked," he wrote his son. Then it grew back. He chalked the hooves on one horse. "That worked," he wrote his son. Then the chalk wore off. Finally the son got a letter that said, "I've figured out how to tell them apart. The white one is two inches taller than the black one." That's what step one is about, the insanity of alcohol and how blind it makes us to sometimes obvious solutions. Most offenders don't even get that message—Step One—from the State.

The first step is the only one that has to be done 100 percent. If you dam a river 99 percent the dam *will* break. Surrender. One hundred percent. That's AA's program, a formula that works for most, but not all, to get to and stay on the right half of the chart.

Did I mention it is free?

Getting irritated at the State bureaucracy for not seeing this seemingly simple solution is easy. However, we are the only republic in the world to keep the same form of government, the same basic constitution, the same bureaucracy for the last 200 years. Regional wars and periodic deep economic recession show that we can get our bureaucracy to line up enough able minds to change a lightbulb from time to time. If Alcoholism and Alcohol Abuse are the public health priority we claim, we need to spend our money on distinguishing the differences between the two, treat each accordingly and save where we can. We need to change the lightbulb.

Chapter Eight

"It isn't the caboose that kills you, it is the engine."

—*AA saying*

JANUARY 6, 2007 and JANUARY 17, 2007

I didn't give myself the advantage of AA immediately after the airport incident. When my wife returned after her three-day hiatus and served me with papers, I was thrown out of the house. I kept drinking, too. Through Christmas and the New Year 2007. Patti suggested we "talk." I was already into my second liter January 6 at 10 a.m. when I dinged a pickup truck passing by as I turned into the liquor store to buy more. I no longer held back on my driving, since Patti was leaving me no matter what. I didn't think twice about driving on after dinging the passing vehicle because it didn't seem that bad. The location outside of a popular liquor store got me pulled over fairly quickly and adding Hit and Run to another drinking and driving arrest. This time, I was booked and held until I made bond two days later.

I got violently ill while detoxing in jail, but I had enough benzodiazepines behind bars to keep from serious withdrawal. The first appearance for this case, also in the same county, was combined with the first appearance for the last case and scheduled for January 30. I drank as soon as I got out.

Eleven days later, I don't recall why Patti was still speaking with me, but I was heading back from her house (our house) on the same highway as the other two tickets. It was January in Wisconsin so it gets darker earlier. I was on my third bottle of whiskey . . . the bottle the officer found in the passenger seat after I put the car in a ditch. A concerned passerby called it in to the county sheriff. This was a "one-car accident" (huh?) on a snowy road. I declined the roadside tests, which I knew I'd flunk and blew a .29 BAC—almost four times the legal limit. I posted $2,500 the next morning and was released after my first appearance. I was pretty desperate for a stiff drink as I had almost sobered up.

Not one of these arrests was unfair, not even unlucky. I was intoxicated.

And I wasn't quite at bottom yet. The disease was raging unchecked.

CHAPTER NINE

"You don't pee in a Mr. Coffee and get Starbucks."

—Unknown

Making the distinction between Alcohol Abuse and Alcoholism may not be something the State pays particular attention to, but insurers sure do. If there was not a crystal clear difference between the two, insurers would not pay benefits for treatment.(If the health policy even covers it, but fortunately most do these days). As we begin an era of mandated healthcare coverage, more problem drinkers and people with drinking problems are going to be entering your insurance pool, whether public, private or employer plans.

Alcohol's costs to insurers is greater than just covering treatment—coerced or not. Alcohol is the number one cause of home, work and recreational accidents according to the National Safety Council. Alcohol is present in 25 percent of drownings. And the American Medical Association credits alcohol misuse with increased probability of heart, brain, liver and pancreatic illnesses. Ten times higher rates of cancer are attributed to alcohol consumption. The two-year California Teachers Study noted the only dietary factor associated with an increased rate of breast cancer was alcohol ingestion, which increased risk by 50 percent. Evil second-hand smoke only increases risk by 27 percent. Cirrhosis is commonly thought of when people think of alcohol related illness or death, but, while cirrhosis is lethal, more Alcohol Abusers and Alcoholics die from alcohol related heart disease. Almost four times as many. Eighty percent of pancreatitis is related to alcohol use. Esophageal damage. Stomach ulceration. Colon disorders. Kidney malfunction. Depressive diseases. All have increased incidence in those who use alcohol.

Alcohol kills, not just when it mixes with gasoline and is the pressure point we can most control if we are to get a leash on healthcare costs. One example of the lethal nature of booze is that there is a high rate of suicide in chronic Alcoholics, which increases the longer a person drinks. This is believed to be due to alcohol causing physiological change of brain chemistry, as well as social isolation. Suicide is also very common in adolescent alcohol abusers, with 25 percent of suicides in adolescents being related to Alcohol Abuse. Approximately 18 percent of Alcoholics commit suicide, and research has found that over 50 percent of all suicides are associated with Alcoholism. (Less than the number and percentage of fatal auto accidents caused by Alcoholism.) The suicide figure is higher for adolescents, with Alcohol Abuse or drug use playing a role in up to 70 percent of suicides.

With heart disease hospitalizations alone representing a major drain of hospital resources and insurance dollars, how much another person drinks absolutely is your business. The Journal of the American Medical Association puts the stats this way: 15 percent of outpatients, 30 percent of inpatients and 60 percent of trauma/ER visits admissions are alcohol related. Alcohol misuse contributes to cholesterol problems, arrhythmia, high blood pressure, lowered immunity, ulcers, hiatal hernia, fractures and osteoporosis, necrosis of the femoral head leading to hip replacement, hypoglycemia, hyperglycemia, stroke, dehydration, avitaminosis and congestive heart failure. And, tragically, Fetal Alcohol Syndrome.

Two years of wading through human excrement on both sides of the law, I quickly saw that the people with jobs and mortgages and degrees and kids don't want anything to do with antisocials, not even to laugh at them on Maury or curse them on the 10:00 news. They take the joy out of public parks, the safety away from our malls and the decency out of just about anything public people enjoy in public because that is what they want to do. Alcoholics belong here, belong lumped in together with Abusers?

They end up here because most Americans don't make the distinction between Abusers and Alcoholics. We see them both as Alcoholism, out of a lack of effort to educate about the difference. But we also see them both as Alcoholism because we see in Alcoholism what we want to see in Alcoholism: Our beliefs cloud the truth and the facts. This problem dates to the Women's Christian Temperance Union (WCTU) in 1874, which worked for a decades preaching on the moral decay caused by alcohol until alcohol was prohibited by the Consititution in the early part of the 20th century. To the WCTU, if you were not a total abstainer, you were a drunkard. Use meant abuse meant Alcoholism. That flawed belief exists today even though the WCTU and Prohibition have been out of our culture for three generations. Alcoholics are still "bad guys."

As an interesting side note, we also have Prohibition to thank for the way we consume our alcohol in the United States. Drinking fast—slamming drinks—and drinking every drop became normal in the years of Prohibition because you didn't want to get caught. And those consumption habits stuck.

Alcoholism is a disease found in six to eight percent of the population. The disease is not in the bottle or in the imagination, it is biochemically in the person. The disease starts with a genetic predisposition to getting the disease. Alcoholism therefore is a physiological disease. If you add alcohol in the life of a person with the genetic predisposition discussed here, you are not guaranteed an Alcoholic however. But consider if you never introduced alcohol to the vulnerable system, you would never get an Alcoholic. Alcohol therefore is the catalyst for the Physiological disease of Alcoholism. If alcohol is never introduced into this flawed physiology, Alcoholism never occurs. It is Occam's Razor: When you have multiple possibilities the simplest solution is always the correct one. Without Alcohol, there is no Alcoholism. Other contributing factors to the disease are social pressure and psychological stress. People without the genetic predisposition, without the Physiological factors, still encounter the same social and psychological stresses, and do not succumb to the disease of Alcoholism (Delta, Gamma or Epsilon types) because they lack the physiological makeup that causes the disease. These people may abuse alcohol and never actually be an Alcoholic.

For starters, the Alcoholic has a genetic flaw where the liver uses Catalase to metabolize alcohol instead of an enzyme known as ADH or Alcohol Dehydrogenase. Evidence supports the fact that when ADH is deficient, the Alcoholic burns alcohol more efficiently than sugar and nerve tissue prefers the alcohol molecule over the sugar molecule. We're talking about something organic here, something we are born with: You can't choose to which enzymes are present and working in your body.

Think of it this way: About eight percent of the population is born without a digestive enzyme Asparaginase. This enzyme breaks down asparagus and makes your urine stink after you eat asparagus. So eight percent of the population doesn't stink when they pee after eating asparagus. They were born that way. They don't get to choose their enzymes either. Eight percent of the population also has the genetic anomaly in the enzymes that will lead to Alcoholism.

Another way to look at it: About eight percent of the population is born left-handed.

Mayflies are even more primitive than we are. The male lives for a couple hours, is born without mouth or stomach, lives just long enough. Why? Why are some left handed? Why are some without the stinky pee gene? It happens. It is neither good nor bad. It just happens.

The other half of the physiological disease is a naturally occurring imbalance in brain chemicals, or neurotransmitters. Dopamine and Serotonin are the Big Two. Dopamine tells the body we need something. Serotonin tells our bodies we have had enough and are fine.

This balance between the Big Two goes back to our prehistoric days. The Big Two regulate our most primal of instincts in what is called the Limbic System, the oldest part of the brain consisting of the amygdala, hippocampus, septum and nucleus accumbens. The Limbic System regulates functions essential to our survival. Dopamine and Serotonin are there to be the on/off switches for self preservation. If we're cold the Limbic System causes us to shiver and decreases blood flow to the extremities. So we know we could die if we don't remedy the situation. The Limbic System regulates testosterone and estrogen so we breed. The Limbic System is the control center for the things we needed, primitively, for survival: Eat, Reproduce, Don't Get Eaten.

Dopamine activates behavior by focusing our body on the signals it gets. When you're hungry, dopamine surges, tells us we need, and creates discomfort in the body, imbalance, until we act on that survival need. When the survival need is met, Serotonin is increased. When the Big Two are neither in correct proportion to each other nor at adequate levels overall, the body reacts to try to balance them. As a system, the human body strives at all times to be at balance. Some of us are just born out of biochemical balance in the Limbic System from the get go.

Backing up a half-step, Alcoholics are born without the enzyme ADH and their body prefers the alcohol molecule. Once the body is introduced to the alcohol molecule and functions better with it, it then desires alcohol and sends a message to the brain saying, "I need something I am not getting." Dopamine increases.

Enter the imbalance between the Big Two. There isn't enough Serotonin to counter the Dopamine at a resting state. Now the body is spiking the Dopamine even higher because it needs the alcohol for survival. Even when the body has enough alcohol to burn because the Serotonin levels are so low to start, they never reach a high enough level to counter the Dopamine, to tell the body it is fine. The Alcoholic's brain tells him, "I still need more in order to survive."

What compounds this even greater is that when the body begins to withdraw from alcohol, that physical pain also triggers more Dopamine to be released because we feel our survival is in danger. So we want even more alcohol, even when the alcohol is what made us feel crummy to begin with. It is a vicious feedback loop. If we just don't have enough Serotonin to begin with as a baseline compared to our Dopamine, or if we don't produce enough Serotonin in response to the Dopamine surges, our body will always be fighting for balance. It's primal, in the oldest part of our brain.

Alcohol is a central nervous system depressant. Use of alcohol *in an Alcoholic* will continue on a binge until the central nervous system becomes so depressed you pass out. There is not enough Serotonin to tell the body it is ok. The Dopamine keeps telling the body it needs more and is unopposed. It is for this reason that an Alcoholic doesn't know that other people do not feel the way they do when they drink and other people ("normies") don't feel the same way an Alcoholic does when he drinks.

To complicate matters even further, some researchers theorize the alcohol molecule itself triggers release of more Dopamine. The chemical composition of alcohol is so close to many neurochemicals that it could mimic or interfere with them especially because alcohol is absorbed directly into the bloodstream at the small intestine without digestion or metabolization.

The balance between the Big Two is not new ground. It was originally discovered in 1992 that obesity could be managed by combining Fenfluramine (which blocks the brain's ability to reabsorb Serotonin) with Phenteramine (which increases Serotonin and decreases Dopamine). The Fen-Phen combination also proved effective in treating Alcoholics in 1993. The Fen-Phen combination however proved to be saddled with side-effects and fatalities and Fenfluramine was pulled off the market.

Rats have the same primitive structures in their brains and the same Big Two. Rats who have had Serotonin removed from their brains have compulsive sexual activity and eating (Eat, Don't Get Eaten, Breed) because there is nothing to counter the Dopamine surges telling the body a survival need isn't being met. If you have hunger, fear or an unconsummated sex drive, that represents Big Two imbalance. The imbalance stems from nothing you do or eat. A neurotransmitter responsible for the balance called Gamma Amino Butyric Acid (GABA) is controlled by your genes.

The physiological disease has its foundation in the genetic deficiency of the low or missing ADH enzyme PLUS the imbalance between the Big Two. What's morality or character or behavior got to do with that? Where does willpower begin to fix that? An Alcoholic is no more capable of willing that physiological picture to correction than a starving person can will himself to a full stomach.

A study was published in May 2010 by the Collaborative Study on the Genetics of Alcoholism (COGA) and funded in by the National Institute on Alcohol Abuse and Alcoholism, the National Institutes of Health and

—

Indiana University. It identified a DNA sequence in chromosome 11 that increased the risk for Alcoholism. This isn't the end-all-and-be-all of the genetic technology and unbiased approaches to determine a root cause, but it bears out that there is a lot more at work in an Alcoholic than bad choices.

In 2008, COGA also indentified a DNA variation in chromosome 4q contributes to the variability of Alcoholism from person to person. Some have an early onset, some have less severe symptoms etc., and in their research COGA scientists found this variability in the disease is rooted in this particular gene. What we've definitively discovered in the genetic research is that these microscopic areas in two microscopic chromosomes have more to do with Alcoholism than bad choices do. If you put alcohol in a body under these conditions, you are at risk. Period. No therapist—good or poorly hired—is going to lecture your genes into compliance. You started your wild shuttle ride from a faulty launch pad.

One reason this chapter on the science of alcoholism is so long is to prove a point. And the point is: Where in this discussion of the body's use of alcohol does the word "behavior" appear. Alcoholism clearly is not a behavioral problem. It is biochemical. The Stone Age didn't end because we ran out of stones. It ended because we evolved. We took what worked and took what we learned most recently and did something with it. Why then is the State still in the Stone Age in the treatment of Alcoholism when we have all these new stones?

CHAPTER TEN

"Oh, the noise! Noise! Noise! Noise!
That's one thing he hated! The NOISE! NOISE! NOISE! NOISE!"

—*"How the Grinch Stole Christmas," Dr. Seuss*

I was raging in my tissues but was fighting to feel normal and the only way I felt normal was to keep that BAC over .10. I knew I was sick, but terrified of drying up. I kept drinking because my body and my brain, (the very organ that could get me better, was the one telling me to drink more) kept saying, "Go," not, "Stop." I knew after that most recent arrest I was not going to avoid jail time. That environment, which I had never experienced, was no deterrent. An Alcoholic who is not afraid of what the alcohol is doing to him, isn't going to be afraid of a jail. Personally, I've seen all kinds of power . . . met seven presidents . . . have two ex wives . . . almost died a couple of times . . . been a minority . . . been in an f/a-18 going 600 mph . . . presented to boards on Wall Street. Prison was not intimidating enough to deter me. (Until now.)

Now I was facing a dog pound—very accurate in likeness on sound and smell—in which the inbred pit bulls prance and nip and bark incessantly. Not everyone sees the environment as being as bad as I perceive. There is a whole culture of people who thrive in this environment. They know a lot of other inmates, their friends and family from the streets or from previous prisons and prior sentences. They know the guards. They know the game. I'll advance the idea that prison is NOT the hardest place for the hardest criminals and the most toxically antisocial: Prison is hardest on the people with morals, family values, education and professional lives. For the hard criminals, this is fun and laughter and free. Decent hardworking people instead . . .

> . . . lose their homes. Some antisocials actually gain shelter by getting locked up. In Wisconsin many get re-arrested for petty street crimes in Sept. and Oct. to avoid winter!

> . . . lose nutrition and health. In one week's menu, we are served 28 slices of bread. And soy. And lots of turkey. Lean wholesome foods are not on the menu or the canteen, but for the harder types, they may actually be eating better on your dime!

> . . . lose contact with family and friends. This is especially true in facilities which restrict phone privileges.

> . . . are used for peacekeeping. If a cell or section of a dorm is involved in illegal activity or just general unruly behavior, the staff moves an educated, mature white guy into the cell or area to poison the mix.

> . . . are used for their education and kindness. If you have more than a GED, you become a resource all day. "Spell this." "Let me ax you something." "Give me that." "Read this and tell me what to do." No please or thank you and especially no excuse me. The hustlers use you up. And everyone is hustling.

I trusted generally. I was certain to help out when someone "axed" me, as well. But I had to shelve that eventually for most of the two years because being a good guy made me prey. THAT frustrated me . . . angered me . . . when it made my heart hard like that.

Every soul here has a story or is a story: A huge, complicated scandal and conspiracy story that begins with their lack of guilt (not their innocence) and continues with a dark saga of some of the bleakest parts of American society. It's their society. The horrors are told semi-articulately in some form of English. The tales last all day and are repeated endlessly.

I had sometimes heard that jails and prisons were full of people who, despite committing the most appalling of crimes, looked like little league coaches or church elders or the guy next door. Must've been the wrong prison. Maybe one in 100 was like me. The rest looked like monsters with broken teeth and dead eyes. There is this segment of population that braided hair and face and neck and hand tattoos may be an OK expression but I have yet to see a pastor or little league coach or neighbor that thought so.

As awful a place as it is, the environment just is not a deterrent. Not for people who like living this way. It isn't much of a deterrent for the six or eight percent of us who have Alcoholism either because, if we have no fear of drinking ourselves to death, prison isn't going to scare us too much. However, had I known, I can't say for certain I wouldn't have become Alcoholic but I sure as hell would have never driven intoxicated. What we see on the documentaries and news specials and programs like "Locked Up" (which is popular on MSNBC for some reason at the time of this writing) showing overcrowding and ridiculous behavior in prison yards and cell blocks is only what they *can* show. Multiply that 10-fold, add stench and imagine that Jerry Springer is the only cable channel program you get and you have to watch it from an uncomfortable steel backless chair wearing bad clothes and you're only getting warmer.

Almost every conversation is vulgar, laced with the N-word and motherfucker. Talk centers on guns, drugs, crimes, booze and victimizing someone, usually a woman. Eating, sleeping and all bodily functions are done in plain view of staff and other offenders. In close quarters. Quarters are so close in fact that a Tuberculosis test is required at least every 13 months and staph infections are rampant.

If you don't like rap, stay out of here. To say all schizophrenics are violent sociopaths is out of bounds. But the connection that rappers, known for violent antisocial outbursts, are also schizophrenic isn't such a leap. Rappers rhyme things . . . schizophrenics rhyme things.

The toilet and shower rooms are the only common areas without cameras, which made for people not flushing, not washing, and also made the bathrooms a hangout for exchanging contraband outside the view of the guards. Criminal contraband, like drugs, and jail contraband, like canteen items you lost in a gaming debt, since it was against the meta rules to possess canteen you did not personally order. So what better place to exchange food products than in a germ playground like the washroom?

The food is as hideous as the hygiene. And it is made by and served by the same inmates who didn't wash and haven't cut their fingernails since Al Gore was relevant.

Did I mention the stench? As a reporter I've covered discoveries of a body or two in the Dallas, Texas summer heat. You don't forget that odor. The smells of prison (bad food, bad body odor, bad breath, unflushed toilets and general filth and decay) is as memorable and second only to those experiences of decomposing flesh.

The handling of inmates is as foul as the air. In my opinion, it only creates the thought that they can use their freedom licentiously and ruthlessly when they are released because they were mishandled in the system.

Luckily for the taxpayer, most states do not have intoxicated-drivers-only prisons. Most don't even segregate the OWI offenders from the general population at all, so the OWI's don't cost you more to house, just more to "treat." You might want to think about that next time you drive anywhere close to the limit. Sleeping in a nine-man cell ten feet from a schizophrenic convicted of substantial battery who stopped taking his meds so he can work in the community is scary far beyond the reality of the 9-to-5 world.

You don't get much rest if you are accustomed to living a 9-to-5 existence in the real world. With the lack of sunlight and exercise, food tearing up your insides nightly, and the nightly noise and bed checks and snoring, the occasional fight and half of the 98 fluorescent bulbs in the dorm burning all night, you just don't rest. Each and every morning you feel like a lumpy, tattered mattress that's been thrown down a flight of stairs and dragged to the curb.

Imagine trying to sleep in a crowded foreign shopping mall paved in feces during the Christmas rush. Bright lights. All the noise but nothing intelligent or intelligible. Huge crowds. Half trying to sell you bologna and the other half trying to steal it from you and all of them in need of a shower and a Tic-Tac. And in this mall you can forget about Starbucks or Orange Julius. Oh, you lost your keys, so you cannot leave either.

Morality and conscientiousness have to be programmed back into a person along with a positive attitude and a smile upon release from this kind of environment if you possessed them before coming in. If you didn't have these things, or if that foreign mall doesn't sound half bad, or if all your pals are in with you, prison might not be so awful to you. This is not normal. However some just thrive on it.

As for the environment, being locked up does suck. It is supposed to. Anything you ever read or heard about the noise, the horrible hygiene, the dirt, the bugs, the racism, the violence, the hustlers, the jailhouse preachers who found God only when the handcuffs snapped shut, the drugs and the atmosphere of disrespect is absolutely true. You will never ever believe it could be this bad. Ever.

Racism is both latent and blatant. I heard a lot of people claim to be colorblind and I know that was only said in the hope of acquiring some good or service. I quickly learned that Viktor Frankl—in "Man's Search for Meaning"—was absolutely correct in saying, "There are only two races in this world: Decent Man and Indecent Man. Both are found everywhere, any group will have both and there isn't a pure race of either." It just happens that the Indecent outnumber the Decent 50-to-1 in jail. And if that makes me racist, I guess I will always root for Team Decent.

The language is as extreme as the boredom: I heard motherfucker 112 times in one single hour. I counted. Why? Because there literally is nothing else to do.

It is a desperate, dirty place. Too much so for me. The intellectual black hole into which I had fallen also was crushing. We're talking about people who get in fistfights over the TV to watch cartoons, wrestling, "COPS" (to see what gets perps caught), "Divorce Court" (to see the single women) and "America's Most Wanted" (to see who they know). The intellect and social skills of the typical inmate are where we were 100,000 years ago. They are us, minus 100,000 years of evolving. This is a sadistic, nihilistic, misogynistic culture you'd like to believe does not exist anymore. The very fact you could read this book differentiates you from "them" because it is found in a part of the library most prisoners never visit: The inside.

People do not get sick of telling the same stories over and over of the same drugs and the same crimes, the same women they do not have and the same money they never had. But they never tire. New lows and more repetition fill nine hours between "quiet times" which is merely a cue to rewind the same thoughtless tape and turn it up only if the guards aren't paying attention. The deep spiritual and moral darkness surpasses even the vacuum of intelligence.

Duty is doing what is right no matter the cost. A job is doing it for cost. Most inmates haven't had either duty or a job. I may not be the only one with a career to ever be locked up. Nor will I be the last. However, I may be the only one to find it so unbearable that I clenched my jaw daily biting back the emotion so hard that I actually cracked a molar.

It got so final for me a couple times that I'd actually considered writing a farewell message to my kids. Parts of it comprise sections of this book. These weren't suicide notes. I was only convinced I'd have an aneurysm any day due to the stress, boredom and anxiety I'd accumulated inside of me. Willpower alone probably prevented that pulmonary catastrophe not to mention a major mental meltdown. I had the kids photos and their phone calls to bridge over some really black days. I knew I'd get out soon. Without that promise, who knows. Being in prison for a person with a conscience creates a whole-body wound. Your spirit is battered. You're physically punished. Mentally you are deprived. It is a deep "being" wound.

CHAPTER ELEVEN

"Comparing the two is like comparing the lightning bug with lightning."

—*Mark Twain*

I was not wounded, did not feel that desperation, after going through rehab before going through hell. I had rested thanks to rehab and got a start on recovery before jumping into my sentence. Until science figures out how to reset the Big Two levels overall and in relation to each other, rehab—legitimate multi-disciplinary treatment, not coerced programs designed for antisocials—is the Alcoholic's greatest hope for learning to live with the disease. You will lose if you fight alcohol, but your odds are pretty good if you learn to exist with it instead of being destroyed by it. There is no Service Pack 2.0 for the genetic/enzymatic/neurochemical software that keeps an Alcoholic an Alcoholic, but the multi-disciplinary approach actually can impact the Big Two imbalance. Meetings (AA and others) can increase Serotonin. Meditation results in a rise in Serotonin. Helping people (the 12th Step of AA) can produce a "helper's high" which increases Serotonin. Prescriptions can also increase Serotonin or reduce the reuptake of Serotonin (so the blood levels of Serotonin remain higher). Stress management reduces Dopamine releases.

Punishment, incarceration and behavioral programs do not have these interests in their design.

Dopamine is produced by "systemic" stressors, like thirst, cold, or a need for the alcohol molecule in bodies that burn it more efficiently. Dopamine can be triggered by "processed" stressors, too, though. These are produced in your mind. Guilt and worry are two processed stressors. Awareness of what these two feelings are and how they can trigger an Alcoholic into drinking is a primary focus of rehab and recovery. Recovery is about balance—personal and neurochemical. This balance is vitally important because for an Alcoholic who has the physiological composition outlined earlier, sobriety is also a stress because the body still prefers alcohol and isn't getting any.

Sobriety therefore can also be considered a diseased state.

Symptoms of Sobriety after the acute withdrawal symptoms disappear include:

> Low self-esteem
> Poor sleep
> Cravings
> Isolation
> Diminished memory
> Emotional sensitivity
> New habit formation (e.g. smoking, candy, etc.)

Rehab treats these symptoms of Sobriety, not just the symptoms of Alcoholism. Untreated, Sobriety will lead right back to relapse. The Minnesota Model of treatment acknowledges this and is recognized as the most effective of treatment modalities. Minnesota Model first treats the acute, medically, because Alcoholism is a disease. Then focus is placed on treating the Sobriety, using the 12-steps. You address guilt and shame. You address the people/places/things that can trigger a relapse. You focus on routines that can reduce the Big Two imbalance. You focus on abstinence as the only goal. Controlled drinking is not an option when you have the disease: It can and does work for many Alcohol Abusers, but there isn't a credible treatment protocol for Alcoholism that has controlled drinking as a goal.

Rehab is about retraining. Cross your arms in front of you right now. Look down. Which arm is on the top? Right over left? Now cross your arms again, but reverse it. Put your left over your right. Feels odd, doesn't it? That is what rehab is about. Taking the same body and doing something different with it that may not feel comfortable at first.

The Criminal Justice system is full of painters when it comes to rehabilitating Alcoholics. The real world's treatment process, where there are active participants in the recovery process—the ones where participants are not coerced—is full of eye doctors. A painter lets you see the world *as he sees it*. An eye doctor will let you see the world *as it really is* more clearly.

You need that clarity to live with Alcoholism. You also need learn how to make relationships work better, not just the ones between the police and your antisocial self.

You learn how to leave behind the toxic ones. That's one thing the Criminal Justice programs cannot even touch. Why? Because the environment itself is toxic.

The Minnesota Model is also big on dealing with loss and regaining respect for yourself. I had a poisonous relationship with image and money. Even more poisonous than the two failed marriages. Alcohol is a solvent and one of the things it is really good at removing is your money. I miss the money I EARNED. Only a liar says he doesn't. The Criminal Justice system prefers to focus on ill-gotten gains, not careers and incomes. But I can make more money. I lost respect and that's hard to make. I lost self-respect and the respect of others. Rehab focuses on that. The Criminal Justice system operates from the baseline that you are not worthy of respect because you are a criminal first, human second. At the end of the day, I can live without the material possessions. I cannot live without the respect for myself and the respect of others. Where the Criminal Justice treatment goes dreadfully wrong is that their view is that you are assumed antisocial because you have been found guilty. You add up the things in your life to see if you are greater or less than the sum of your parts and if—in the State's view—one of your parts is Alcohol Abuse, the sum will never add up to the positive no matter what you've done. Is this the message on which you want your dollars spent?

The State's way doesn't work because it skips all these "human" components in the most sub-human environment. A three-year recidivism tracking of offenders in 1999 found that 42 percent of those participating in these tough-love-and-tough-shit programs returned to alcohol and prison within three years. This is *exactly* the same as the recidivism rate for those who didn't do the programs. (The Austin, Tex. Criminal Justice Policy Committee conducted the landmark research.) That is the most telling evidence that you spend all that program money year in and year out with no measurable result.

Effective rehabilitation focuses on problems (not labels), surrender, acceptance and the amplification of the positive aspects of you and your life. The Minnesota Model and the 12 Steps are not the only way to get that. Before you get anything, you have to get the alcohol out of your system. Quitting "warm turkey" won't do it either. Whether you are fed crap with a spoon or a shovel, it is still crap. Quit. And detox safely.

Effective treatment includes a support component, too. It doesn't matter which support program is best or first or biggest. The Oxford Group predates Alcoholics Anonymous. These two groups are our original Chat Rooms! Rational Recovery was all the rage briefly in the 1990s for anti-12 Steppers. There's Self Management and Recovery Training (SMART). There's the Secular Organization for Sobriety (SOS).

Social Skills Training is successful, on the *outside*. It teaches the skills in dealing with or getting a job, working with family, choosing friends and self-/emotional-control . . . none of which are fostered in a Corrections environment. Family therapy works . . . but what do you take away in the Corrections environment? Family. Instead we put the offender next to someone who is an Abuser, not an Alcoholic. Motivational therapy works because it is one on one. In Corrections, MY/YOUR goals are irrelevant and to focus on the individual rather than the collective is interfering with the goal of Corrections which is to warehouse.

Community Reinforcement Approaches (CRA) are taught among the larger Correctional systems. They view Abuse only, and Abuse as a result influenced by social or economic factors such as communication, problem solving, job search, finding better friends, recreation counseling (WHAT?) and family goal-setting. This has been proven successful on the outside, where one-on-one counseling with a therapist can be done. It is not successful in a Corrections environment where one on one doesn't play into the "community" shotgun approach. You cannot and will not be permitted to design your own individual and family recovery for what is a very individual and family disease.

The professionals and paraprofessionals handling the treatment are critical to the success. And to build that success you need credibility, especially because there are so many paraprofessionals affiliated with recovery. It's their duty to adhere to a code of ethics simply not embraced in a Corrections environment. Knowledge and competence—not necessarily a degree—are required, and trust. Who do those with alcohol problems trust? Others who have walked a mile in their shoes. A mechanic isn't a metallurgist even though what he works with is metal, so you still need a multi-disciplinary team including medical doctors or psychotherapists, however having someone who is in recovery helping facilitate the recovery process gets better results.

The most important facet of good treatment is alleviating guilt, shame and grief. We look through life's window which can get coated with a grime of guilt and shame and grief. Those are precisely the three features Corrections uses in their programs to make sure you're sorry, make sure you know you're sorry, and won't do it again. Positivity and attitude are the window cleaner that can clean the window so clearly your beagle bangs into the sliding door in a full sprint thinking the door isn't even there. Corrections won't do windows and won't let you wipe the grime from your own.

Recovery can be spontaneous despite the State's best efforts. It does happen. However, true rehabilitation is based on Opus Contra Naturam—working against what comes easily—and in the State system, you are discouraged against learning how to work against what comes easily and just follow the rules or else. There is nothing to address the need to recover and recover *wholly* (as in the whole person) in the programs taxpayers purchase.

You do find that "whole" in the facilities and rehabs that are a league ahead of coerced programs. And if you checked the math, these private resources are less expensive in the long run than State programs in terms of recidivism and long-term health costs. Glad I had the opportunity to get real rehab before the State tried to suck it out of me, but before I got to rehab in Arizona, I still had one more bottom off of which to bounce.

CHAPTER TWELVE

JANUARY 23, 2007

When I got the third arrest and made bail, I was still intoxicated a couple days later when I caught another drinking and driving arrest January 23, 2007, a mere 41 days after the first arrest.

I was driving, on the same highway again, and at midday again. I put my Escalade in the ditch, another single-car accident. And my last ditch.

As I was being pulled out of the ditch by another driver with a full-size pickup, a Milwaukee County cruiser arrived to check out the scene. He just happened to be on the same road passing in the other direction. I failed all three field sobriety tests and requested a blood test rather than breath, hoping the benzodiazepines would also show up in the blood. That was a mistake, as my BAC was .38 and going *up* when the blood samples were tested. I was held in the Milwaukee County Jail until I could post the $5,000 bail. Only when it was reduced to $1,000—two weeks later when they thought I sobered up—could I post bail and get out of one of the most horribly violent places I had ever seen.

My stunning run was over. Four arrests in six weeks. Plus divorce papers. Detoxing in county jail was physically and mentally crushing, but I was at .00 for the first time in a long, long time. For me, .00 wasn't "normal" any more and my body and brain hurt after barrels of whiskey from June 2005 to January 2007. In a few short weeks I went from being viewed as the perfect obedience school dog, well-mannered, never shit on the floor, to being a rabid and mangy pit bull that chewed through the leash and ran through the neighborhood knocking over garbage cans and eating kids on tricycles.

If I had just made that flight back in December.

Immediately upon release, my Arizona friend hired an attorney for a steep sum, all of it up front. I asked the attorney to stall all the proceedings if he could because I really needed help. Treatment, not just the detox, and not a program. I couldn't do it myself because over time the only thing I proved I could do myself was drink. I doubted myself, and very much doubted I'd stop if I started drinking again. And boy did I want a drink. My body was killing me. The attorney was attempting to consolidate all four cases in one court, a procedural move that would buy me the time I needed for serious rehab. Before the court could coerce me into a program, before I'd let them, I chose the where and what.

I flew to Arizona right away—drank on the plane and at the airport though—and went into Intensive Outpatient Program (IOP). IOP was a temporary solution until an inpatient bed opened up at a residential alcohol facility in Chandler. I knew I was killing myself but figured I had about 365 days before the alcohol did me in. The Chandler and Tempe facilitators suggested hours was more like it. The way I was drinking it wasn't liver disease that would kill me they pointed out, but I could bleed out, or most likely, at the levels of sedation I was hitting daily, it wouldn't have been long before I had a serious household accident or just plain poisoned myself with alcohol. The border between a lethal dose and my tolerance dose was that dangerously thin and I had passed the lethal dose level for most people almost daily.

I detoxed again, the right way this time, with medical supervision. Doctors were concerned about the benzodiazepines more than they were about the alcohol because I wasn't acutely intoxicated when I arrived for the inpatient bed that became available.

On the legal front, the courts did not want to consolidate the cases despite the cost savings, however my attorney expected that result. Drinking drivers are too popular a mark for District Attorneys and judges alike and each wanted a piece of me. My final arrest became the first of the cases to be tried. This was a legal maneuver since the judge in Milwaukee County was notorious for throwing the maximum sentence at drivers and by sentencing guidelines, his maximum sentence for the first of these four would be significantly less than his maximum if I was facing him after being sentenced by three other judges by the time I faced him. It was a good recommendation by a good lawyer to go this route, which is an entirely legal procedural move. The order of the arrests doesn't count, the order of convictions does.

I had several appearances after rehab on each of the cases so I was flying back 1,400 miles almost every other week for "status hearings," which are five minute hearings where all parties are required to attend. More importantly my kids were up in Wisconsin and I needed to see them. Other than them, my home and my support network—including the Intensive Outpatient (IOP) treatment I chose as follow up to my residential treatment—were in Arizona. Six months after discharge from residential, the Milwaukee County judge had a tantrum because he wouldn't be able to give me the maximum six years but only one year because of the procedural move. He wasn't pleased I was in Arizona either, even though that, too, was legal and permissible under the conditions I had imposed on my bail. I got a year. I did eight months of that time in the county jail, two of them on Extended Supervision, which is house arrest, without incident or violation.

House arrest was a bit comical. The county doesn't offer Global Positioning Satellite (GPS) bracelets or Self Contained Remote Alcohol Monitor (SCRAM) bracelets. They insist you have a landline telephone and they call you as frequently as hourly to make sure you are in the house, verifying on that the voice recognition software could determine that my voice was answering the phone. It is so easy to see how a dope dealer or anyone so inclined could cheat the Extended Supervision, and they frequently did.

I was terrified of returning to that county jail so I made damn sure that phone was answered on the first ring and that even at 2:00 or 3:00 a.m. the software could recognize my voice even after being yanked from a dead sleep. When I was released from Extended Supervision for good behavior, I returned to Arizona while the other three cases proceeded, with the same fly-back-for-five-minute-court-appearance routine. And there were a lot of them, because each case had to be amended for the Milwaukee conviction.

Eight months after that county jail experience, I began my sentence for the other three arrests which we wrapped up within weeks of each other. It was time in September, 2008. I'd grown very annoyed at all these status hearings, so I skipped one. That was a violation of my bail and resulted instantly in a bench warrant for my arrest. I thought about running, man did I think about it, after experiencing the filth and noise and violence of my first sentence. I knew that would be the end of being a dad though, living with an open warrant over my head. My stint in rehab showed me that running was not realistic because I fought unrealistic odds to get the help and wouldn't live long on the run without the healing I'd already begun. September 14, I turned myself in to avoid arrest on that warrant. More importantly, by turning myself in I also avoided charges of bail jumping, which only would have made the next sentence more severe.

I would get credit for the time served while I waited in jail for the remaining convictions. My first arrest—the one that happened before the airport incident at the start of this book—became my next conviction in October 2008. I got only probation for that conviction, even if my BAC was higher and even though I rearended a Jetta in that arrest and I only hit a ditch in the Milwaukee conviction. By any measure of fairness or consistency or common sense, I should have gotten probation for the *first* of the convictions, not this one. I'm not complaining. This sentence was also to be imposed concurrent to the next two upcoming, so essentially I was given a break by a judge who acknowledged the extreme circumstances of my life at the time I made these mistakes, and I was given credit for making such a tremendous commitment and cash layout to get treatment.

In November 2008, my second to last arrest became my third of the convictions. I received 18 months sentence, also concurrent to whatever my next sentence would require. In December, the second arrest became my last conviction. Procedurally, it made sense to expose this arrest to the potential sentence guidelines because it was the least severe of the BAC levels in the four arrests and the judge with the most knowledge of Alcoholism as a disease not a behavior. I received 24 months, concurrent to the other sentences.

Oh yeah, I also had fines, but the courts just took all the bail money paid and that covered all but $2,878 of the fines.

Now that I finally faced all the sentencing judges, two years following the first of the four arrests, I was removed from the county jail and sent to prison for the remaining sentence time.

I plead guilty to each case. There are no plea deals in drinking and driving in Wisconsin. You plead guilty or go to trial. A trial would have been at taxpayer expense and an enormous expense at that because there would have been four since the DAs and judges refused to consolidate the cases. This expense was unacceptable because I really did drive after drinking. I was responsible and just wanted to get this over with. I took the initiative to get well again, and I made certain to plead guilty to be accountable for what I did. I may have a disease, but until we start cursing the condition instead of punishing the person, I had to own up to the punishment for my traffic violations.

Eight-hundred-fifty thousand dollars. That's my personal estimate of the financial damage from lawyers, cars, fines, rehab and almost three years of not being permitted to work. That's punishment that doesn't quit. I won't get that back, just like I didn't get a re-do on the next 24 months of my life. YOUR bill for my room and board, medical care, transportation and healthcare for my children plus the income and property taxes I'm not paying in that 24 months is another $318,000. Thank God it wasn't worse, because I didn't physically injure anyone. Even myself. Until now.

The tragedy of owning up to my traffic mistakes after already beginning recovery is that I was getting my self-esteem back and I was sober well over a year and I was working a good recovery program, then WHAM I was shipped off to prison. All that work on getting my self respect back and getting past my guilt could be undone by where I was about to go. Prison will rob anyone of the self-esteem that is essential to staying in recovery. And it will rob you of it daily, relentlessly. That's the nature of the prison environment. And the prison programs.

CHAPTER THIRTEEN

"Was mich nicht umbringt, macht mich starker."
(That which doesn't kill you makes you stronger.)

—*Frederich Nietzsche*

I grew up Catholic.

My grade school, Catholic.

My high school, Catholic.

Nuns. Guilt. Mass. Parables of moral living. Catholic. Catholic. Catholic.

The best parable I ever heard? Jewish.

It's called the Tree of Sorrows. (I didn't convert to Judaism or find God or become a Bible-banger or worship the devil while I was locked up, preferring to be mostly agnostic so people wouldn't bug me.)

On the Day of Judgment each person will be allowed to hang all his unhappiness on a branch of the tree. Then, after everyone has theirs on the tree, you can walk around and find a set of sufferings you'd prefer over the ones you hung on the tree. Each man chooses to reclaim his own at the end.

I'd certainly trade off the intense hell I was in for the 20 months I was incarcerated. (I was let out four months early for good behavior.) The "sorrows" I've had as a result of my drinking and my disease, I *would* reclaim off the Tree of Sorrows because I have learned so much through recovery and living day to day with sometimes despair, sometimes breakthroughs and discoveries, sometimes struggling and most times just living with it. I've learned about the science that's being ignored, largely, by the State.

Surrender is still the first place to be. Getting hope of your own free will is a transformingly courageous acknowledgement of a critical problem and the longing for resolution. After surrender, find out about the biochemistry and accept that you cannot alter some of the genetic decisions that were already decided in your tissues and your brain. Finding out what happened isn't going to cure anyone, but it can be a component to staying on the right side of the chart on page 44 and to bringing closure to the damage the disease causes each person individually.

The truth about the disease doesn't set anyone free. The facts do not change the attitudes. There's a story about a hunter stumbling into a strange land where people were living in fear of monsters in the field. The hunter saw it. It was a watermelon. He said, "I'll kill it for you." He slashed it off the vine, cut it open and ate it. Now, people were more terrified of him than the monster and they ran him off thinking the hunter would kill them all next. Another stranger comes into the land and instead he agrees with the villagers that it was a dangerous and terrible monster problem. He gained their confidence by *sharing* the fear. Slowly he taught them the facts about melons and they soon cultivated them.

We're scared of this monster, Alcoholism, but we also remain attached to generations of opinion that say good people with good homes and good families don't get this bad disease, therefore it must also be true that people with the disease don't deserve good homes and good lives and good families. Even if we are talking about eight percent of our population. Treat the antisocials who drink as antisocials. Treat the people who want treatment with legit treatment, not mistreatment. Permanently end the abuse of programs by conmen who aren't really Alcoholics by screening the blood sample given at the time of an arrest for OWI for the following indicators of Alcoholism:

- Gamma Glutamyl Tranferase, a liver enzyme
- A complete blood count to measure the size of red blood cells and number of white cells

- Carbohydrate-deficient Transferrin, a carrier of iron in the blood
- Organ and liver function
- Serum Magnesium, which is below baseline in Alcoholics
- High levels of Uric Acid, Folate and Protein.

We already have these tests and the blood. USE THEM to keep anti-socials from scamming tax dollars and earning release to work dorms or to the streets by falsely qualifying for programs. These tests are the canary in the coal mine. Why aren't we using them? The BAC test is useless as a determinant of anything other than the present rate of alcohol in a driver, not the presence of a disease or a personality disorder. Use the blood for these nine exams, which collectively can indicate the presence of a long-term drinking problem, not just a problem drinker.

Better yet, END driving after drinking—not just reduce it but end this 100-percent—by mandating Ignition Interlock Devices on all cars just like we mandate seatbelts. You are still going to have to wear your seatbelt and I strongly advocate that because there are drivers high on THC (weed) and opiates that never get tested or questioned because the probable cause doesn't show up on a field breathalyzer.

Spend less on the antisocials and more on research for the disease and prevention of Alcohol Abuse and, for God's sake, hold your elected officials accountable for the results they do not have for coerced programs that do not work. Since its formation in 1971, the National Institutes on Alcohol Abuse and Alcoholism repeatedly demonstrate to legislators that for every $1 spent on treatment, $3 in benefits are returned to our nation, yet we still cut that $1 to shreds and spend a lot of it on people without the desire (or even the need) to abstain. The State has shot an arrow and has drawn the target around it: If you are convicted of drinking and driving or any offense even remotely associated with alcohol, their meta rule is that you are required to take the program you pay for as a taxpayer. Bad treatment isn't only tolerated, it is the norm and in my estimation it scares off a trip to "good" treatment or more effective treatment for many. Bad is NOT better than no treatment at all. Especially when your tax dollar is on the line. If you are paying for this, I'd gladly sell you shares of a verdant pasture in the Sonoran Desert which boasts crop circles, a crashed UFO and Elvis sipping from a natural spring of bubbling ice cold cola. Ask for proof of what you are buying.

If you aren't an Alcoholic but love one, leave it alone at first even if that sounds contrary to logic and begin with yourself. You are sick, too. You hide his booze or dump it out, it is a waste of time and money because we will find a way to drink until the alcohol says it is time . . . you get him to promise, well we lie about drinking when we are drinking . . . you tell us to man up and use our willpower and—honest to God—we're already overwhelmed with guilt and shame because we tried to quit behind your back and failed . . . you tell us to do it for you or the kids, just know that the understanding of this chemistry disease in Chapter Nine and the Limbic System (eat, don't get eaten, procreate) overrides how much a man truly loves a woman or his kids because for the seven or so percent of us, we are surviving by drinking not by quitting.

Alcoholics, make your amends though. You said some really awful stuff and didn't mean a lot of it when your tissues screamed at you. That's no excuse for being an asshole. And don't touch things you have no business touching once you accept you are an Alcoholic. The results do NOT change. You know, it is like your lawn. Mow it. Do what you can. A weed seed may blow in from time to time, but you can uproot it rather than letting it take over. A stray dog may crap in your lawn but you pick it up and move on instead of letting it become part of your lawn and the dog part of your life. You do not have any business with weeds or dog poop when it comes to your lawn . . . you don't have any business with alcohol when you are an Alcoholic. You wouldn't tolerate it if your lawn was dying: YOU are dying so stay away from the stuff that's killing the lawn of you.

If drinking was really better than not drinking, I wouldn't have bothered with this book.

Man can change the world when possible and himself when necessary, and we sure can fix the Abuse vs. Alcoholism challenges facing healthcare and society because it is possible, necessary and easy. There are a ton of clichés and sayings to address this problem the U.S. has but I think it comes down to the following four:

1. You have to be in the cave to see the writing on the wall. Pretending Alcohol Abuse and Alcoholism are the same is going to bite our economic butt. And programs posing as counseling and posturing to know how either functions will continue to be a painful economic reality.
2. Getting help beats getting dead. If you are an Alcoholic, you will not be in recovery if you are going to insist on being the Lone Ranger.
3. Don't call a plumber to fix the electric. The criminal justice system has no place in helping those who want help.
4. Staying sober is easier—and less costly—than getting sober. I mean that personally as well as professionally. You cannot recoup the cost—ask for a refund—for an ill-ly administered State program, nor can you hope for anything resembling recovery, only compliance . . . if that.

Gaining ground in treating our watermelon of a monster involves knowing the science and the myths of the disease and its treatment, getting the right people the right help, and getting our National priorities aligned toward reaching goals of reducing Corrections expense, preventing 85,000 preventable deaths a year and helping people with the capacity to be the Early Bird to regain that capacity rather than showing them What the Early Worm Gets.

"I was cured all right."
The last words of Alex in the U.S. version of "A Clockwork Orange," Anthony Burgess, 1962

Learn more about lapse
relapse and Symptoms of Sobriety
in
"Every Silver Lining Has A Cloud"
NEW from Scott Stevens in 2012